hi
God,

it's me again...

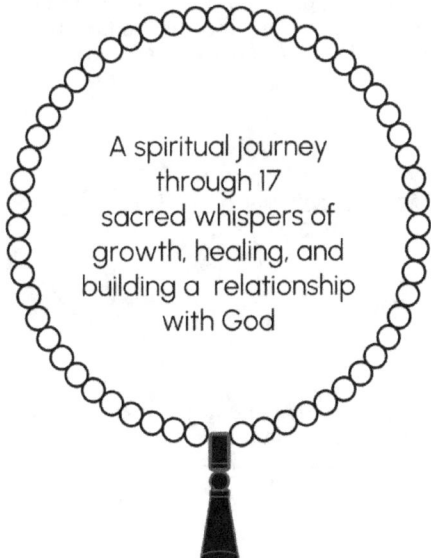

A spiritual journey
through 17
sacred whispers of
growth, healing, and
building a relationship
with God

Brother Reza
Abu Rasmieh

hi God, it's me again...

ISBN Paperback: 979-8-9930783-9-7
ISBN Hardcover: 979-8-9930783-8-0
ISBN E-Book: 979-8-9930783-7-3

Cover design by Brother Reza
Self-published by Brother Reza

This book is a work of reflection and fictional storytelling, inspired by real-life experiences. Names, characters, places, and events are either imagined or thoughtfully adapted for narrative purposes. Any resemblance to actual persons, living or deceased, or to real events is entirely coincidental.

Printed in the United States of America
First Edition

For permissions, inquiries, or correspondence, please email:
email.brother.reza@gmail.com

Acknowledgments

To Allah, The Most Loving, The Most Near

To You belongs all praise. You are the source of my breath and the destination of my longing. You opened my heart, steadied my steps, and taught me how to return, again and again. You let my prayers find their way, even when I didn't have the words. You taught me, even as a child, how to speak to You, how to turn questions into whispers, and silence into connection. You allowed me to see that my imperfection was Your perfection, proof that even my flaws were stitched with mercy. For every miracle whispered into being, this book is my thank you. I love You.

———————— ✺ ————————

To my beloved Prophet Muhammad ﷺ

You showed me/us how to adore, remember, and love God, not through fear, but through gentleness. In your example, I found the language of devotion and the beauty of surrender. For that legacy, my heart bows in eternal thanks. I love you.

———————— ✺ ————————

To my Mother

This book carries your fingerprints, on every prayer you whispered, every tear you hid, and every sacrifice you made. You held my dreams like sacred trust, taught me the whisper of prayer, and gave me the courage to speak to God, both in the beginning, and in the becoming. Your love was the first language of mercy I ever understood. You showed me that devotion could be quiet, and strength could wear a gentle face. This book is my thank you, and may you receive its blessings. Thank you for loving me as I am. I love you.

Table of Contents

Letter to the Reader Page 1

Chapter 1: Where the Friendship Begins Page 4

Chapter 2: A Whisper That Reached Heaven Page 10

Chapter 3: Come As You Are, Leave Loved Page 16

Chapter 4: Light on the Tongue, Heavy with Love Page 22

Chapter 5: Gratitude in Stillness Page 28

Chapter 6: The Grace of Letting Go Page 34

Chapter 7: When Prayers Breaks the Silence Page 42

Chapter 8: Between This World and the Next Page 48

Chapter 9: My Heart in Your Hands Page 56

Chapter 10: The Home of My Regret and Reliance Page 62

Chapter 11: By His Name, I Begin and Trust Page 70

Chapter 12: You are Enough for Me Page 76

Chapter 13: What Words Cannot Hold Page 82

Chapter 14: Not Even for a Blink Page 88

Chapter 15: Just You, God . Page 94

Chapter 16: The Way Back Page 102

Chapter 17: Glory and Praise Page 108

Letter to the Reader Page 114

Letter to the Reader

Dear Reader,

Before anything else, I want to begin with gratitude to Allah, the Most Loving, who gave me the courage, clarity, and strength to write this book. This has been a labor of love and longing, shaped not by scholarly credentials but by life itself. It has been formed through its stumbles, its sweetness, and its sacred whispers.

I do not claim expertise in the Quran or hadith, and I am not an Islamic scholar. What qualifies me is something simple and sincere. It is my love for Allah, for the Prophet Muhammad ﷺ, and for Angel Jibreel. This love grew through my own struggles and imperfections, and it led me to the reflections I share in this book.

Hi God, it's me again is not a formal manual. It is a spiritual companion. Within its pages are 17 chapters, each anchored in a dhikr, a daily remembrance of God, and each paired with three short stories meant to help you reflect on your own journey.

These stories explore themes like love, loneliness, surrender, gratitude, identity, and healing. My prayer is that somewhere in these chapters, you'll find a moment, a voice, or a struggle that feels familiar. That you'll whisper, "That sounds like me," and allow that realization to draw you closer to Allah.

This book is written through the lens of my faith in Islam, but its heartbeat is universal. It carries the desire to speak to God honestly, lovingly, and often. Wherever you are in your spiritual journey, whatever tradition you follow,

I believe these reflections, supplications, and stories can offer you peace, presence, and perspective.

You can speak to Him from the heart and call Him by the name that feels closest to you. You might reach for Him in prayer, silence, music, nature, or even in moments of doubt. All of it is welcome. That's okay.

If your heart is seeking something deeper, this book is here to sit with you. Not to instruct, but to accompany. The language between you and God should be unique and personal to your relationship with Him. Your words to Him don't have to be poetic or perfect. Just honest. That is enough.

I believe dhikr is more than ritual. It is therapy for the soul. In this space, Allah is the One who listens patiently and without judgment. He understands your wounds and your tiredness, your hopes and hesitations, your tears and your silence. More than anything, He desires a friendship with you. Yes, a friendship. Not formality. Not perfection. Just friendship. A bond built on honesty, vulnerability, and return.

I offer these supplications not as prescriptions but as an invitation to find healing, hope, and honesty with God.

As you read, you'll notice I use God, Lord, and Allah interchangeably. I've included references to His holy names where they felt meaningful. Whenever the Prophet Muhammad ﷺ is mentioned, I've chosen to include the symbol ﷺ as a soft invitation to offer salawat, a prayer of peace and blessings in his honor. Carrying that same feeling forward, many of the hadith I've shared are ones that spoke deeply to me. I hope that what touched my heart might speak to yours as well.

While the Arabic language offers many transliterations, I've intentionally chosen those that feel gentle on the tongue and clear to the ear. These are pronunciations that invite you to speak with ease and comfort. Because I want you to truly understand the meaning, you'll find that some of the translations from Arabic to English have been thoughtfully adapted. Not to stray from the core meaning, but to make the spiritual essence more personal while still honoring familiar and accepted interpretations.

May Allah bring clarity to what the heart longs to express and open every heart that reads to receive it.

Let yourself be present.
Take a deep breath.
And begin:

> Hi God, it's me.
> Maybe for the first time, or maybe again,
> but it's still me.

Chapter 1
Where the Friendship Begins

I love you
I love you
I love you, Allah

Dear Friend,

Some dhikrs rise from the depths of longing. Others flow from the ease of trust. Then there's this one, so simple it might slip through unnoticed. In truth, it carries the weight of devotion.

> I love You.
> I love You.
> I love You, Allah.

It doesn't seek permission. It doesn't follow formality. It simply reaches, like a hand toward light, like a heart remembering where it came from.

Love for Allah isn't measured by precision, but by presence.

So how do we begin?

This dhikr is not a request. It's a heartbeat.
Say it when you're far or found.
Say it when you're aching, when the world feels dim.
Say it when you're joyful, when you're laughing.
Say it when you're lonely or loved.
Say it when you're full of gratitude.
Say it when words fail, but love remains.

Let yourself be present.
Take a deep breath.
And begin:

> Hi God, it's me again.
> I'm new to this. I just want
> to say...I love You.

✹ A Stroll Through Time

He walked slowly, matching her pace. His mother's grip was delicate, two fingers wrapped around his hand, familiar yet fragile. The same hand he used to clutch as a child, when her steps guided him. Now, he guided her.

Side by side, the world seemed to pause around them. He looked down at her and whispered:

"Mama, I love you more than love, and I never want you to forget this love."

She looked up, her eyes twinkling through years of sacrifice and prayer. Her face, adorned with gentle wrinkles, told stories of lullabies, late nights, and faith.

With a smile soft as dua, she replied, "I love you more, more than love. You must never forget."

That evening, he sat on his prayer mat, heart full. He repeated the words, not to her this time, but to the One who gave him her love in the first place:

I love You.
I love You.
I love You, Allah.

For him, this dhikr was not just devotion. It was gratitude, for every step beside her, and every breath stitched with love. Now, in the later chapter of her life, he carried the blessing of being her caretaker. He offered back the joy and ease she had so often given, yet rarely received. Each repetition held her presence, and the joy of serving the one who had once carried him, and in return, serving God.

❂ A Grandfather's Grace

Her grandfather, Sedo, knelt slowly beside her. Sara's small hands curled into his, eyes wide with joy.

He looked at her with tenderness stitched into every wrinkle and whispered, "I love you, sweetie. More than love, and I never want you to forget this love."

Sara beamed, ear to ear. Pure and unfiltered. "Sedo, I love you more. More than you love me."

That evening, Sedo bowed his head in prayer, repeating the same phrase. This time, he spoke to the One who had gifted him such moments.

> I love You.
> I love You.
> I love You, Allah.

For Sedo, the dhikr wasn't a ritual, it was reflection. Of all that was good. All that was tender. All that was divine.

❂ The Womb's Whisper

Mariam sat, fully present to the moment, one hand on her belly. The child was still on the way, but her heart was already full.

With a soft breath and a heart full of wonder, she whispered, "I love you. I love you more than love, and I never want you to forget this love, my baby."

Her baby shifted.
A subtle movement.
An acknowledgment.

In her imagination, she heard and felt the reply: 'I love you too, Mommy. More than you love me.'

That night, Mariam sat in prayer and whispered,

I love You.
I love You.
I love You, Allah.

For Mariam, whispering those words felt like planting a seed of love inside her, one she hoped would grow into her child's personal love for Allah.

❁ · ❁ · ❁

Dear Friend,

Love holds a beauty words cannot capture, yet none shines more brightly than the love we hold for God. The Messenger of God ﷺ reminded us that divine love is not distant. It is near. Not earned through perfection, but drawn close through sincerity, remembrance, and love.

So we begin with love. This dhikr is not a request. It is a reaching, a tender offering from the heart to the One who shaped it.

Embrace Allah with every fiber of your being, and let Him become the Love at the center of your soul. Whisper to Him, without hesitation, and He will remind you, in ways only He can, that He loves you too.

It is through this infinite unfolding that you discover the Friend who understands your silence, your tears, your puzzled thoughts, and your laughter.

It all begins with a single intention, a trusted step forward. Before the second step is even taken, you will find Him already there, welcoming you with unconditional love. Just as you are.

Let yourself be present.
Take a deep breath.
And begin:

> Hi God, it's me again.
> I just want to say I love You,
> yes again.

Chapter 2
A Whisper that Reaches Heaven

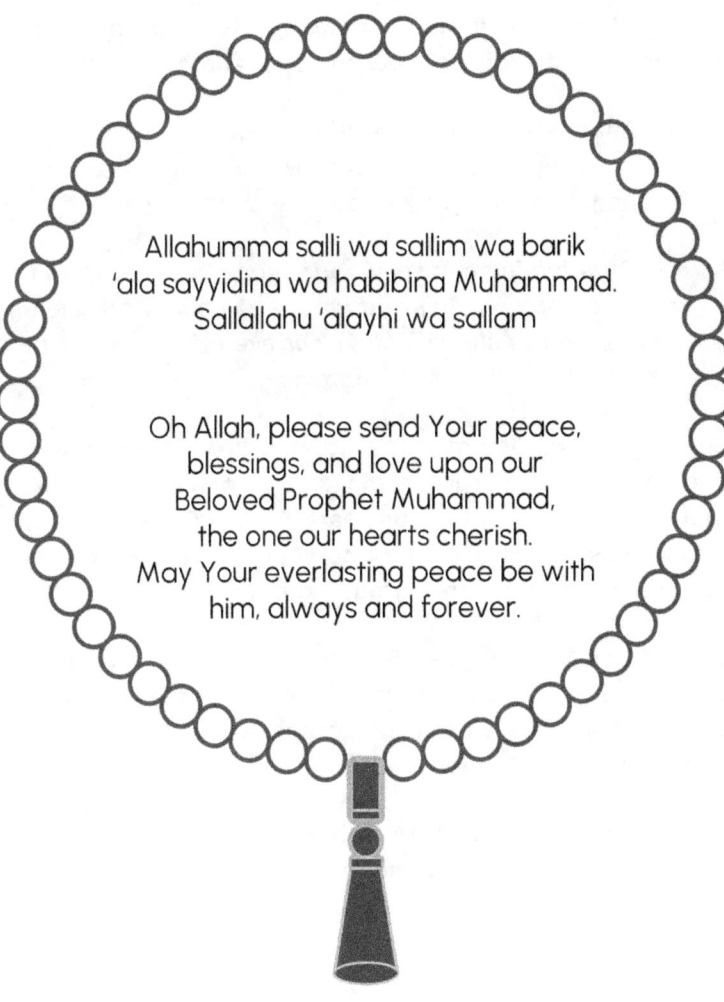

Allahumma salli wa sallim wa barik
'ala sayyidina wa habibina Muhammad.
Sallallahu 'alayhi wa sallam

Oh Allah, please send Your peace,
blessings, and love upon our
Beloved Prophet Muhammad,
the one our hearts cherish.
May Your everlasting peace be with
him, always and forever.

Dear Friend,

Following the dhikr of love for Allah, we turn to a prayer of love for the one who showed us the way to Him. Through the Prophet Muhammad ﷺ, we learn how to worship, how to forgive, how to hope, and how to heal.

Allahumma salli wa sallim wa barik
'ala sayyidina wa habibina Muhammad.
Sallallahu 'alayhi wa sallam

Oh Allah, please send Your peace, blessings, and love upon our Beloved Prophet Muhammad, the one our hearts cherish. May Your everlasting peace be with him, always and forever.

Sending salawat is not just a ritual. It is a prayer of love and peace for the Prophet ﷺ. It is a pause in time. A moment to recalibrate your heart. A way to invite mercy, forgiveness, and divine love into your life. It is a whisper of devotion that echoes through the heavens.

Say it when you feel lost. Say it when you feel grateful. Say it when you want to remember that someone once walked this earth with perfect compassion, and that his legacy still lives in your heart.

Allahumma salli wa sallim wa barik
'ala sayyidina wa habibina Muhammad.
Sallallahu 'alayhi wa sallam

Oh Allah, please send Your peace, blessings, and love upon our Beloved Prophet Muhammad, the one our hearts cherish. May Your everlasting peace be with him, always and forever.

❀ The Grandmother's Wisdom

A grandmother sat, gazing at her grandson who had grown into a young adult. She saw the weight he carried: sadness, confusion, a kind of pain that lingered beneath the surface. Her instinctual wisdom, shaped by decades of life, stirred within her.

"My dear Anas," she said gently, "I've lived through joy and sorrow. Each wrinkle in this hand you're holding, each line on my face, carries a story. Some born of laughter. Some carved by sadness. Even the deepest ones, my dear, were etched by depression.

Anas looked at her, surprised by her honesty. She had spoken a word their culture rarely named, depression. She spoke it with dignity, not shame.

"I know what it feels like to carry something heavy in your heart," she continued. "Whether you find yourself in joy or in sorrow, in clarity or confusion, remember this prayer:

Allahumma salli wa sallim wa barik
'ala sayyidina wa habibina Muhammad.
Sallallahu 'alayhi wa sallam

Oh Allah, please send Your peace, blessings, and love upon our Beloved Prophet Muhammad, the one our hearts cherish. May Your everlasting peace be with him, always and forever.

Recite it often. It will ease the burden in your chest."

She placed her hand over his heart and whispered the prayer aloud, letting the words settle between them, gentle as a lullaby singing to the soul. The grandson nodded, tears forming. That night, he began reciting the salawat daily. Not as a cure, but as a companion. A way to feel seen. A way to feel held.

For him, salawat became a lifeline. It was a bridge
between pain and peace, a reminder that he is, and has
never been, alone.

✺ The Friends Who Chose Grace

Two childhood friends, inseparable since they could walk,
found themselves in the middle of a painful argument.
Words were sharp. Emotions raw. Years of closeness felt
like they were falling apart.

They had shared everything: birthdays, heartbreaks,
dreams. Yet now, tension hung heavy in the air, and
silence felt like a wall between them.

In the heat of the moment, one of them paused and softly
said, "Salī 'ala Muhammad." It wasn't a command. It was a
plea. A gentle reminder to send peace upon Prophet
Muhammad ﷺ.

The other friend looked up, surprised. They both fell
silent. It was in that stillness that they recited together:

> Allahumma salli wa sallim wa barik
> 'ala sayyidina wa habibina Muhammad.
> Sallallahu 'alayhi wa sallam
>
> *Oh Allah, please send Your peace, blessings, and
> love upon our Beloved Prophet Muhammad, the one
> our hearts cherish. May Your everlasting peace be
> with him, always and forever.*

The anger didn't vanish instantly, but something shifted.
The salawat softened their hearts. It reminded them of
the Prophet's mercy, his patience, his love for
reconciliation.

They forgave. They hugged. Then they moved forward, not

because the issue was forgotten, but because love had been remembered.

For them, salawat wasn't just a prayer. It was a path back to each other. A sacred pause that turned conflict into compassion.

❁ The Father's Faith

He sat quietly in the living room, holding the roles of husband and father, with the weight of losing his job pressing heavily on his chest. Bills were piling up. His children needed him. Even then, he didn't know how to tell his wife that he felt like he was failing.

He remembered his mother's voice from years ago. She had once told him, "When life feels heavy, send blessings upon the Prophet ﷺ. His remembrance has a way of lifting the weight within."

So he began. Every morning. Every night. Every time anxiety crept in, he whispered:

> Allahumma salli wa sallim wa barik
> 'ala sayyidina wa habibina Muhammad.
> Sallallahu 'alayhi wa sallam
>
> *Oh Allah, please send Your peace, blessings, and love upon our Beloved Prophet Muhammad, the one our hearts cherish. May Your everlasting peace be with him, always and forever.*

He didn't see results immediately. Still, he felt steadier. He felt guided. He remembered the Prophet's teachings, "Allah will never burden a soul with more than it can bear." "With hardship comes ease." "What is meant for you will come. What is not meant for you will pass."

He found peace not in answers. He found it in presence.

Weeks later, he found a new job. It wasn't glamorous, but it was enough. He could provide, he could breathe, and he could finally look at his children with gratitude instead of guilt.

For him, salawat didn't erase the struggle. It became a way through it, turning hardship into healing, and fear into faith.

❈ · ❈ · ❈

Dear Friend,

Salawat is a gift. A way to love the one who loved us before we were born. A way to connect with the mercy of Allah through the mercy of His Messenger.

Say it when you feel distant. Say it when you feel close. Say it when you want to remember that you are part of a legacy of love.

Let yourself be present.
Take a deep breath.
And begin:

> Hi God, it's me again. I just want to send love to the one who taught me how to love You. Bless him. Elevate him. Let his light live in my heart. Through him, I found a path back to You. A way to feel held. A way to feel home. So I turn to You now, with love in my heart and his name in my prayer.

I submit to You and I declare:

> Allahumma salli wa sallim wa barik
> 'ala sayyidina wa habibina Muhammad.
> Sallallahu 'alayhi wa sallam
>
> *Oh Allah, please send Your peace, blessings, and love upon our Beloved Prophet Muhammad, the one our hearts cherish. May Your everlasting peace be with him, always and forever.*

Chapter 3
Come As You Are, Leave Loved

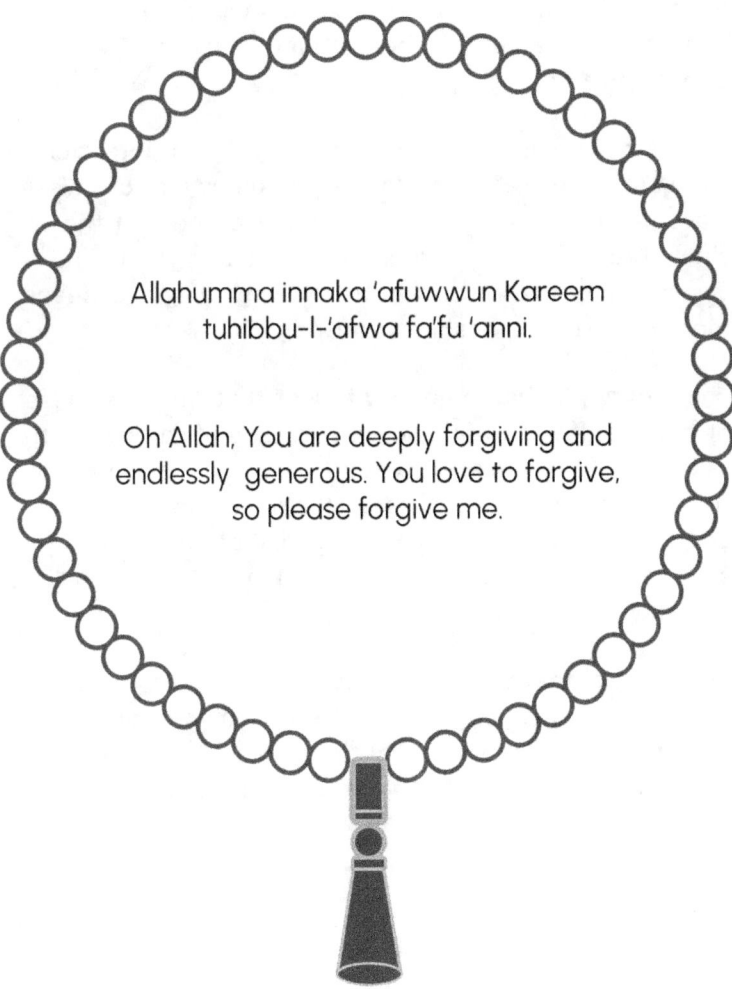

Allahumma innaka 'afuwwun Kareem
tuhibbu-l-'afwa fa'fu 'anni.

Oh Allah, You are deeply forgiving and
endlessly generous. You love to forgive,
so please forgive me.

Dear Friend,

This dhikr is a doorway to mercy. It is a heartfelt plea from a heart that knows it has faltered, yet still dares to hope. It's for the one who feels ashamed, the one who longs to be clean again, the one who whispers, *Please, God, forgive me.*

We are flawed and forgetful. We trip over our intentions and sometimes return to the very habits we swore we'd leave behind. Still, have you ever considered that the very sin you regret might be the path that leads you to the sweetness of faith? It could be the beginning of a deeper, more honest relationship with God.

The Prophet Muhammad ﷺ taught that the sweetness of faith begins to unfold when even one of three qualities takes root in the heart. These include a love for Allah and His Messenger that surpasses all else, a bond with another that exists solely for the sake of Allah, and a sincere desire to stay away from sin after God has helped you leave it behind.

Think about that third trait. The pain of regret, the desire to change, the longing to never return to what once broke you are signs of a heart awakening. Allah knows your story. He knows what led you there, and He loves when you turn back to Him.

Let yourself be present.
Take a deep breath.
And begin:

> Allahumma innaka 'afuwwun Kareem
> tuhibbu-l-'afwa fa'fu 'anni.
>
> *Oh Allah, You are deeply forgiving and endlessly generous. You love to forgive, so please forgive me.*

Say it with hope. Say it with humility. Say it knowing that God is waiting. He is not here to punish, but to pardon. Not here to reject, but to rebuild. Not here to turn away, but to welcome.

❁ The Mother's Prayer

A mother spent countless nights waiting by the window, hoping her daughter would return home safely. Her child had begun staying out late, drifting into a world the mother didn't understand. She worried. She wept. She questioned herself, wondering what she had done wrong.

Each night, the daughter would enter softly, greet her mother, and head to bed. One evening, though, the mother couldn't hold her sorrow in. She fell to her knees in prayer, tears streaming down her face.

"Lord, please guide my child. I worry for her. Please, Allah, forgive her. Forgive us." She repeated the dhikr over and over:

Allahumma innaka 'afuwwun Kareem
tuhibbu-l-'afwa fa'fu 'anni.

Oh Allah, You are deeply forgiving and endlessly generous. You love to forgive, so please forgive me.

Unbeknownst to her, the daughter had entered and stood silently behind her, watching her mother's desperate plea. Something stirred. The daughter knelt beside her, whispering the same words:

Allahumma innaka 'afuwwun Kareem
tuhibbu-l-'afwa fa'fu 'anni.

Oh Allah, You are deeply forgiving and endlessly generous. You love to forgive, so please forgive me.

The mother turned, surprised. "What brought you here?" With tears in her eyes, the daughter said, "Mom, I want to change. I need to change. This time, I will change."

They embraced. Then together, they entered sujood, with foreheads to the ground and hearts lifted to heaven, repeating the dhikr as a shared prayer for forgiveness and renewal.

For them, repentance wasn't a private act. It was a bond. A return to Allah, hand in hand.

✹ The Young Man's Turning Point

In his mid-twenties, Idris carried a hidden love for Allah. It was a love that lived deep within him, one he felt only he and Allah truly understood. Even with that love, he found himself entangled in temptation, committing sins that left him feeling hollow.

After each slip, shame would flood his heart. He'd ask himself, "How did I let this happen? How did I choose this over my relationship with Allah?"

One night, overwhelmed by guilt, Idris performed two rak'ahs of Salatul Tawbah, the Prayer of Repentance. In sujood, he wept and whispered:

Allahumma innaka 'afuwwun Kareem
tuhibbu-l-'afwa fa'fu 'anni.

Oh Allah, You are deeply forgiving and endlessly generous. You love to forgive, so please forgive me.

He made a promise to himself before Allah, pledging never to return to that sin.

A year later, Idris reflected on that night of his return. He remembered the sin, the pain, the prayer, the promise. That very sin, he came to understand, had led him to the sweetness of faith. The shame and regret had become a path to a renewed relationship with his Lord.

For Idris, the dhikr wasn't just a plea. It was a turning point. A moment that transformed shame into sincerity.

❂ One Step Toward Him

In his mid-seventies, Bashir sat quietly in the masjid, reflecting on a life filled with both joy and regret. His youth had been reckless. His adulthood, careless. Now, in the stillness of old age, he longed for peace.

He remembered his thirties, a time when he felt lost and unsure how to change. At a community gathering, an elderly woman named Sumaya had taken his hand and said, "When I was your age, I was broken. Then I found Allah, and with Him, I found purpose. Take one step toward Him, and you will know you're not alone."

Bashir had asked, "But where do I begin? Will Allah forgive someone like me?"

She smiled and replied, "Begin with this and say it with sincerity. Say it until your heart believes it:

Allahumma innaka 'afuwwun Kareem
tuhibbu-l-'afwa fa'fu 'anni.

Oh Allah, You are deeply forgiving and endlessly generous. You love to forgive, so please forgive me

That night, Bashir began his journey. He reached out to those he had wronged. He asked for forgiveness. He made amends. He made this dhikr part of his return to God.

Years later, sitting in the masjid, he felt something he hadn't felt in decades. Peace. Not because his past was erased, but because his heart was finally at rest.

For Bashir, forgiveness wasn't just divine. It was transformative.

❀ · ❀ · ❀

Dear Friend,

Wherever you are in your journey, whether young or old, broken or healing, remember this. Allah loves you. His mercy is vast. His forgiveness is near. There is no sin too great, no mistake too deep, that He cannot forgive.

Change begins with intention. With a whisper. With a dhikr.

Let yourself be present.
Take a deep breath.
And begin:

> Hi God, it's me again. I turn to You seeking transformation. I beg You to forgive me for every sin I've committed, whether during the day or at night, in private or in public. knowingly or unknowingly, alone or with someone, whether minor or major. Forgive me, Lord, for my shortcomings, and thank You for concealing them from the eyes of others. I make this dhikr today, tomorrow, and forever, knowing Your mercy will meet me there.

I submit to you and I declare:

> Allahumma innaka 'afuwwun Kareem tuhibbu-l-'afwa fa'fu 'anni.

> *Oh Allah, You are deeply forgiving and endlessly generous. You love to forgive, so please forgive me.*

Chapter 4
Light on the Tongue, Heavy with Love

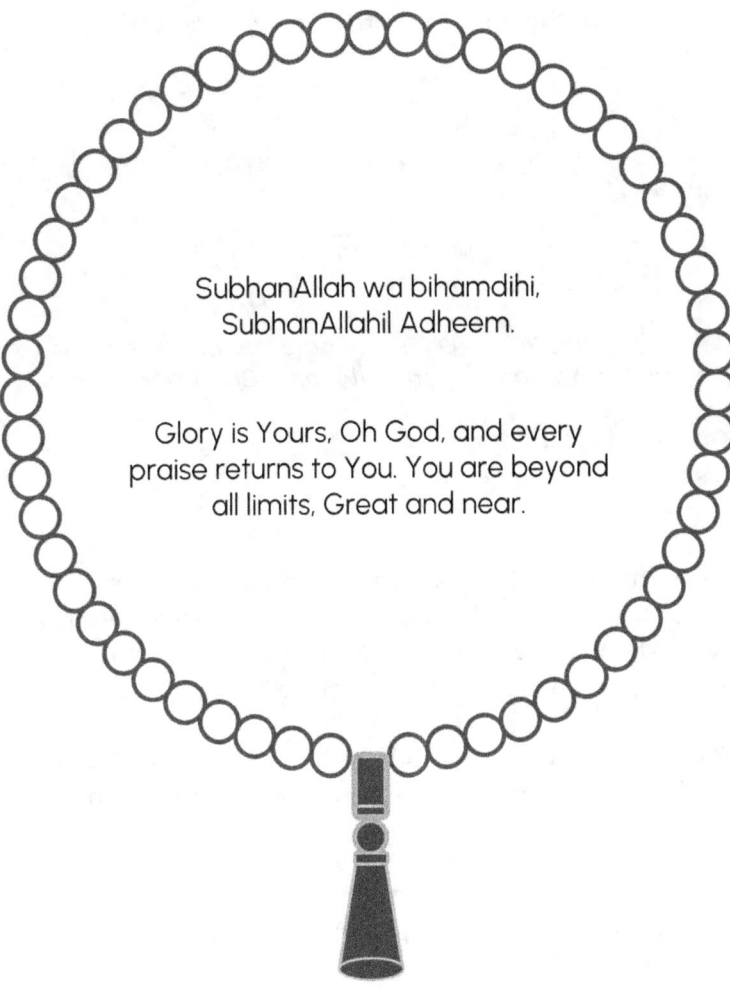

SubhanAllah wa bihamdihi,
SubhanAllahil Adheem.

Glory is Yours, Oh God, and every
praise returns to You. You are beyond
all limits, Great and near.

Dear Friend,

This dhikr is light on the tongue, but heavy on the scale. It's a whisper of awe, a breath of praise, a moment of surrender to the majesty of the One who created everything.

The Prophet Muhammad ﷺ said these words are beloved to Allah, easy to say, yet immense in reward. They are:

> SubhanAllah wa bihamdihi,
> SubhanAllahil Adheem.
>
> *Glory is Yours, Oh God, and every praise returns to You. You are beyond all limits, Great and near.*

This isn't just a phrase.
It's a breath of remembrance.
A seed of eternity.

Each utterance plants a tree in Paradise. It is rooted in sincerity, nourished by the longing of your heart. It grows even when you're tired, even when you're distracted, even when you're just trying to stay close.

Your voice matters. Your remembrance matters. Your love for Allah, however shaky or steady, is never ignored.

Say it when something takes your breath away. Say it when everything feels like too much and you can't find the words. Say it when you want to honor Him, not for what He has done, but simply for who He is.

> SubhanAllah wa bihamdihi,
> SubhanAllahil Adheem.
>
> *Glory is Yours, Oh God, and every praise returns to You. You are beyond all limits, Great and near.*

❀ The Garden of Roses

Amira held her grandmother's hand as they strolled through the park. The sun was soft, the breeze gentle, and the trees swayed like they were listening.

"Tata," Amira asked, using the Arabic word for Grandma, "may I ask you a question?" "Of course, my love."

"Do you think there are trees in heaven with leaves like roses?"

Tata smiled, her eyes twinkling. "Oh, Habibti. Yes, of course. In heaven, there are trees with leaves made of roses. You must plant the seeds now to have them."

"How is that even possible, Tata?"

"Our Beloved Prophet Muhammad ﷺ said that if you fill your tongue with 'SubhanAllah wa bihamdihi, SubhanAllahil Adheem' a hundred times, a tree will be planted for you in Paradise."

Amira's eyes widened. "So I can grow a garden in heaven?"Tata nodded. "Yes, My Love. If you can imagine a tree with leaves made of roses, then Allah can create it for you. It is my prayer that you have a valley of trees with leaves in the most colorful shades your eyes long to see.

From that day on, Amira began reciting the dhikr every morning. Sometimes aloud, sometimes in whispers, sometimes while drawing pictures of rose-covered trees. It became a practice of hope. A way to dream of Heaven while still walking through this world.

For Amira, this dhikr became more than words. It became a dream. A garden of remembrance blooming beyond time.

❋ The Artist's Awakening

Sadiya was an artist who painted in silence. Her canvases were full of color, but her heart often felt gray. She struggled with purpose, wondering if her work mattered, if her voice was heard, if her soul was seen.

One day, while painting a sunrise, Sadiya paused. The light was so perfect, so gentle, so alive. Without thinking, she whispered:

> SubhanAllah wa bihamdihi,
> SubhanAllahil Adheem.
>
> *Glory is Yours, Oh God, and every praise returns to You. You are beyond all limits, Great and near.*

It felt natural. Like the colors themselves were praising. Like the brushstrokes were a form of worship.

Sadiya began saying this dhikr every morning before painting. It became a sacred beginning, a way to let each brushstroke carry something meaningful.

She started leaving small notes on the back of each canvas: "This painting was born from praise. May it remind you of the One who creates all beauty."

As her skill grew, so did her heart. Sadiya began to see the world not only in color and form, but in signs of divine beauty. Dhikr became her lens. Every sunset, every raindrop, every smile became a reason to whisper praise.

> SubhanAllah wa bihamdihi,
> SubhanAllahil Adheem.
>
> *Glory is Yours, Oh God, and every praise returns to You. You are beyond all limits, Great and near.*

For Sadiya, dhikr turned creativity into connection, into presence, into prayer.

✿ The Patient's Prayer

Rayyan rested in a hospital bed, his body healing but his spirit searching for comfort. He felt weak, uncertain, and alone.

A nurse named Zahra entered and adjusted the IV. Her presence was calm, her movements gentle.

"Is there anything I can get you?" she asked.

Rayyan shook his head. "Maybe a little peace."

Zahra smiled. "My grandmother used to say, when you feel helpless, say *SubhanAllah wa bihamdihi, SubhanAllahil Adheem*. It's like breathing something sacred into your sorrow. A way to remember you're never alone in it.

Rayyan began whispering the dhikr. Slowly. Softly. With each repetition, the room felt lighter. Not because the pain disappeared, but because the presence of Allah entered the space.

He began reciting it before every lab test, every treatment, every moment of fear. It became his comfort. His courage. His connection.

One night, Rayyan noticed a mini sundial compass resting on his bedside. He turned it over and found a verse from the Quran etched into the back: Whichever way you turn, there is the Face of Allah. The words settled in his chest, steady and true. They stirred a familiar dhikr: SubhanAllah wa bihamdihi, SubhanAllahil Adheem. For the first time in weeks, he smiled. Not because he was healed, but because he felt held.

For Rayyan, dhikr didn't heal the body. It healed the soul. It reminded him that even in his weakness, he was never alone.

Dear Friend,

This dhikr is a song of praise. A breath of wonder. A way to say, "I see Your greatness, and I am grateful." It's for the artist, the child, the patient, the seeker. It's for you.

Say it when you're surrounded by beauty.
Say it when you're searching for meaning.
Say it when you long to plant something eternal.
Say it when you're healing.

Let yourself be present.
Take a deep breath.
And begin:

> Hi God, it's me again. I just want to praise You. Not because I need something, but because You deserve everything. You are beauty without limit. Majesty beyond measure. Glory is to You. Praise is to You. Always and Forever. I love You.

I submit to you and I declare:

> SubhanAllah wa bihamdihi,
> SubhanAllahil Adheem.

> *Glory is Yours, Oh God, and every praise returns to You. You are beyond all limits, Great and near.*

Chapter 5
Gratitude in Stillness

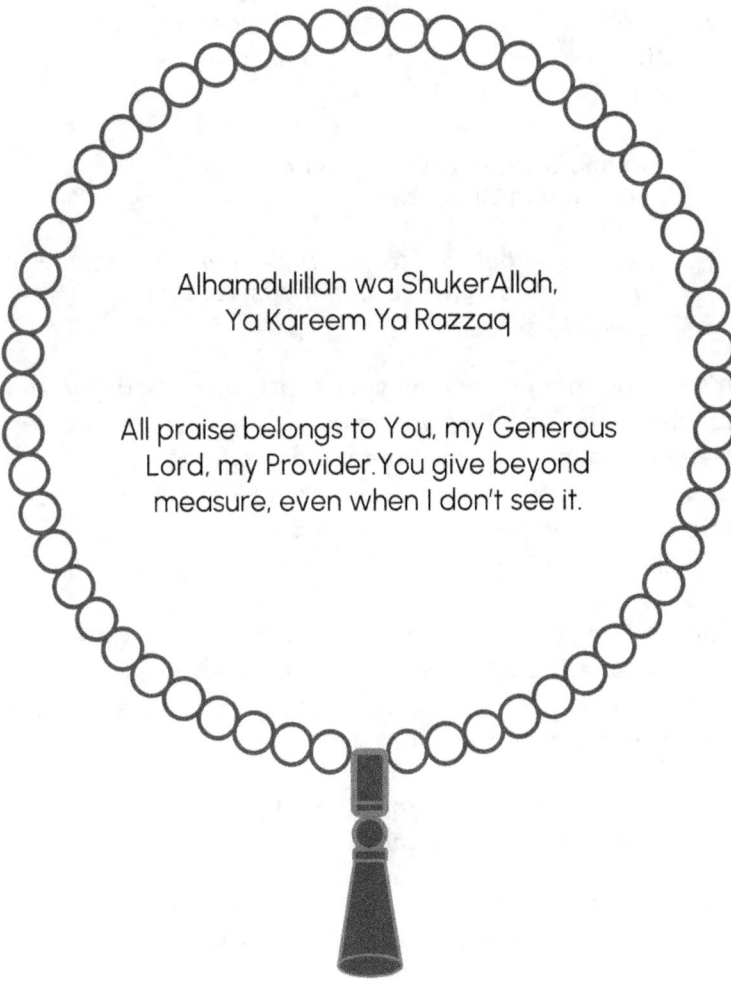

Alhamdulillah wa ShukerAllah,
Ya Kareem Ya Razzaq

All praise belongs to You, my Generous
Lord, my Provider.You give beyond
measure, even when I don't see it.

Dear Friend,

Gratitude is not just a feeling. It's a form of worship. It's the sincere acknowledgment that everything we have, everything we are, and everything we hope for comes from the One who gives without measure. This dhikr is a celebration of that truth:

> Alhamdulillah wa ShukerAllah,
> Ya Kareem Ya Razzaq
>
> *All praise belongs to You, my Generous Lord, my Provider. You give beyond measure, even when I don't see it.*

It's for the moments when your heart swells with joy, and for the moments when you're holding on to hope with trembling hands. It's for the food on your table, the breath in your lungs, the unexpected kindness, and the strength to endure. It's for recognizing that even in hardship, there is mercy.

Say it when you receive good news. Say it when you're waiting for a breakthrough. Say it when you feel forgotten. This dhikr reminds you that you are always being provided for, even in ways you cannot see.

> Alhamdulillah wa ShukerAllah,
> Ya Kareem Ya Razzaq
>
> *All praise belongs to You, my Generous Lord, my Provider. You give beyond measure, even when I don't see it.*

❂ The Baker's Secret

There once lived a baker who found joy in the flow of his craft. His name was Ismail. His bakery was more than a business. It was a sanctuary of warmth, scent, and community. People from across the city would rise early just to taste his bread, which carried not just flavor, but soul.

Ismail's employees admired him, not only for his skill but for his humility. Among them was a teenage girl named Eman. She had lost her father at a young age, and over time, she came to see Ismail as a paternal figure. He never treated her like just an employee. He taught her, encouraged her, and trusted her.

Eman worked with devotion, as if the bakery were her own. She noticed something curious. Several times a day, Ismail would say, "Eman, you're in charge. Give me one minute." Then he would disappear into his office. He'd return exactly sixty seconds later, calm and smiling.

At first, she thought nothing of it. Then one day, her curiosity began to rise.

"Uncle," she asked respectfully, "may I ask you something personal?" "Anything, dear," he replied warmly. "I've noticed you take one-minute breaks throughout the day. I hope it's okay to ask. What do you do during those one-minute pauses?"

Ismail's eyes softened. "May I share a secret with you?" He leaned in gently. "Every time I excuse myself, I go into my office. I place my forehead on the ground in *sajdah*, and I whisper, *Alhamdulillah wa ShukerAllah, Ya Kareem Ya Razzaq*. I thank Allah for every loaf of bread, every customer, every breath. I imagine myself kissing the earth beneath His Majestic Throne, the *Kursi*. I do it not because I need more, but because I already have so much."

She had never seen gratitude practiced like this. Not as a custom, but as a language the soul seemed to understand.

Ismail smiled. "When you pause in the middle of a busy day to thank Him, He sees that love. In return, He offers more blessings than you can count."

For Eman, that moment changed everything. Gratitude became her compass and this dhikr became her morning prayer.

✿ Held Through the Shadows

Qasim often sits in quiet moments, remembering a childhood that left marks no one could see. The home he grew up in was loud with anger, filled with confusion and silence. There were days he felt invisible, and nights he wished he could disappear. Some memories still return uninvited, carrying the weight of words that wounded and moments that never felt safe. The pain didn't come all at once. It arrived slowly, like shadows stretching across the years.

Even then, something held him. Not perfection. Not certainty. Just a devotion to Allah. He didn't always understand his place in the world, but he never stopped thanking the One who had placed him in it.

> Alhamdulillah wa ShukerAllah,
> Ya Kareem Ya Razzaq
>
> *All praise belongs to You, my Generous Lord, my Provider. You give beyond measure, even when I don't see it.*

He whispered it often, sometimes through tears, sometimes through hope. What steadied him most was the knowing that through God's love, change would come. Not all at once, and not always in ways he expected, but gently, in time.

Now in his mid-thirties, Qasim stands in a life he once only imagined *and prayed for as a child*. He is independent. Respected. At peace. He doesn't rely on anyone to define his worth. His dependence is on Allah alone. Each morning, before the world begins to speak, he returns to the dhikr that carried him through.

Alhamdulillah wa ShukerAllah,
Ya Kareem Ya Razzaq

All praise belongs to You, my Generous Lord, my Provider. You give beyond measure, even when I don't see it.

❁ When Anxiety Met Remembrance

Isra had lived with anxiety for as long as she could remember. As a child, she often felt a tightness in her chest before school, a heaviness in her stomach before sleep. She didn't always have the words for it, but she carried it in silence, hoping it would ease with time.

Now, as a university student juggling exams, part-time work, and family responsibilities, that same anxiety followed her into adulthood. Life felt like a constant sprint. She often felt overwhelmed, underprepared, and tired in ways she couldn't always name.

One evening, after a long day, Isra stepped into the campus prayer room. The lights were dim. The carpet was warm. She placed her forehead on the ground and whispered,

Alhamdulillah wa ShukerAllah,
Ya Kareem Ya Razzaq

All praise belongs to You, my Generous Lord, my Provider. You give beyond measure, even when I don't see it.

Something softened inside her. It wasn't dramatic. Just a shift. That night, she began a small gratitude journal. One line a day. I woke up. I had coffee. My friend checked in.

The entries were simple, but they steadied her heart.

Days turned into weeks. Her anxiety didn't vanish, but it loosened its grip. Her prayers felt deeper. Her relationships grew gentler. Life was still full, but it no longer felt like too much.

For Isra, this dhikr didn't erase the pressure. It gave her a way to carry it. Gratitude became her anchor. Her way of staying present, even when everything felt like a blur.

❖ · ❖ · ❖

Dear Friend,

Gratitude is not reserved for perfect days. It's for the messy ones. The slow ones. The ones where you're just trying to hold it together. This dhikr is your reminder that Allah sees your effort, your endurance, and your appreciation.

Say it when you feel full. Say it when you feel empty. Say it when you're not sure what tomorrow holds, but you trust the One who holds it.

Let yourself be present.
Take a deep breath.
And begin:

> Hi God, it's me again. I just want to say thank You. For the things I see. For the things I don't. For the blessings I count, and the ones I've missed.You are Generous. You are my Provider. I am forever grateful to You. I love You.

I submit to you and declare:

> Alhamdulillah wa ShukerAllah,
> Ya Kareem Ya Razzaq

> *All praise belongs to You, my Generous Lord, my Provider. You give beyond measure, even when I don't see it.*

Chapter 6
The Grace of Letting Go

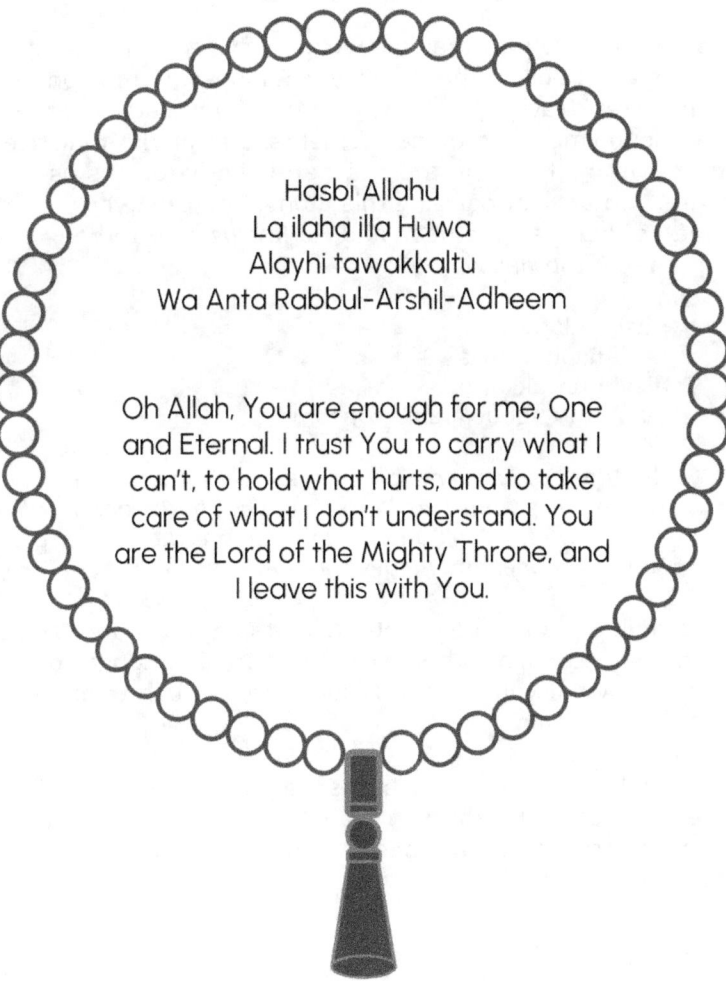

Hasbi Allahu
La ilaha illa Huwa
Alayhi tawakkaltu
Wa Anta Rabbul-Arshil-Adheem

Oh Allah, You are enough for me, One
and Eternal. I trust You to carry what I
can't, to hold what hurts, and to take
care of what I don't understand. You
are the Lord of the Mighty Throne, and
I leave this with You.

Dear Friend,

This dhikr is a companion for moments of fear, uncertainty, and emotional heaviness.

Sometimes we may feel like we're carrying more than our hearts were built to hold. Anxiety. Sadness. Confusion. Loneliness. Maybe you've whispered to yourself, "I can't do this anymore." In those moments, a reminder may rise from within. It lives in the heart and gently returns us to truth. You are not carrying this alone. The One who created your heart is near, and He knows how to hold what feels too heavy.

> Hasbi Allahu
> La ilaha illa Huwa
> Alayhi tawakkaltu
> Wa Anta Rabbul-Arshil-Adheem

Oh Allah, You are enough for me, One and Eternal. I trust You to carry what I can't, to hold what hurts, and to take care of what I don't understand. You are the Lord of the Mighty Throne, and I leave this with You.

This dhikr is not merely a comfort. It is a declaration. God is enough. Enough to hold your heartbreak. Enough to untangle what you cannot understand. Enough to calm the storm within.

Say it when your chest tightens. Say it when the world feels unjust. Say it through tears. Say it with strength. Because trusting Allah doesn't remove the ache. It redeems it.

> Hasbi Allahu
> La ilaha illa Huwa
> Alayhi tawakkaltu
> Wa Anta Rabbul-Arshil-Adheem

Oh Allah, You are enough for me, One and Eternal. I trust You to carry what I can't, to hold what hurts, and to take care of what I don't understand. You are the Lord of the Mighty Throne, and I leave this with You.

❂ Victory in Silence

Sunya had just started her first job as a lawyer. New desk. New title. A fresh beginning. Still, something familiar surfaced: the sting of being unseen, dismissed, doubted, overlooked. It was the kind of dismissal that came not from her work but from who she was. She was a woman, visibly Muslim, stepping into a space that hadn't expected her.

One colleague made her feel small. He spoke with coldness, kept his distance, and often questioned her intelligence behind her back. The tension grew beneath the surface.

The pattern continued. Her ideas were brushed aside. Her efforts ignored. Comments about her inexperience slowly wore her down. Others noticed. No one said a word. Their silence stayed with her.

One evening, sitting alone in her car, she felt the weight of it all. A memory surfaced as her grandmother's voice returned, like a truth she'd always known. When you feel afraid, speak the words that make fear smaller.

> Hasbi Allahu
> La ilaha illa Huwa
> Alayhi tawakkaltu
> Wa Anta Rabbul-Arshil-Adheem

Oh Allah, You are enough for me, One and Eternal. I trust You to carry what I can't, to hold what hurts, and to take care of what I don't understand. You are the Lord of the Mighty Throne, and I leave this with You.

So she began saying it. Quietly in meetings. Softly in hallways. Sometimes under her breath when passing that colleague. She didn't expect the world to change. What she needed was for her soul to stay anchored.

Weeks passed. Then something shifted. The remarks softened. The air around them changed. One afternoon in the break room, he looked up and said, "I've been unfair to you. I'm sorry." Sunya didn't say much in return. She simply nodded and said, "Your apology is accepted." She let the words settle. It wasn't a grand moment. It was enough. Enough to remind her that strength doesn't need volume to be felt.

She didn't fight the storm. She trusted the One who could calm it, control it, and through grace, fight her battles on her behalf.

For Sunya, this dhikr wasn't about finding control. It was about finding Allah in what she couldn't control. He fought her battle for her, and now she could rest. Not in certainty, but in trust.

❀ The Bumper and the Blessing

Asad had just gotten his driver's license. That afternoon, he made a small mistake and tapped the back of another car. No one was hurt. No real damage. Still, his whole body felt unsteady, caught between panic and relief.

The driver stepped out, looked over the bumper, and sighed. "It's nothing. Don't worry. I won't report it."

Asad remained in his car, heart racing, eyes wide. That's when he remembered something his mother had taught him: "When fear unsettles you, say the words that steady your soul."

> Hasbi Allahu
> La ilaha illa Huwa
> Alayhi tawakkaltu
> Wa Anta Rabbul-Arshil-Adheem

Oh Allah, You are enough for me, One and Eternal. I trust You to carry what I can't, to hold what hurts, and to take care of what I don't understand. You are the Lord of the Mighty Throne, and I leave this with You.

He whispered it once. Then again. His breath slowed. His chest softened. The panic didn't disappear, but he had placed it in the care of the One who understands.

Later that evening, he told his mom what had happened. She didn't scold him. She just smiled and said, "You did the right thing. Not just on the road, but in your heart."

For Asad, the dhikr wasn't just a comfort. It was how he found strength. A way to turn a moment of fear into a moment of faith.

❁ The Whispering Ground

Every morning, Yunis sat near the window with a cup of tea and a heart too heavy for its frame. The television played in the corner. Images of his homeland filled the screen. Families displaced. Homes turned to rubble. Children with eyes too old for their years.

His lips moved in silence, not to argue with fate, but to plead with the One above it.

Hasbi Allahu
La ilaha illa Huwa
Alayhi tawakkaltu
Wa Anta Rabbul-Arshil-Adheem

Oh Allah, You are enough for me, One and Eternal. I trust You to carry what I can't, to hold what hurts, and to take care of what I don't understand. You are the Lord of the Mighty Throne, and I leave this with You.

He said it not with anger, but with sorrow. Not for answers, but for nearness. His dhikr was a form of protest. One that surrendered to God what the world could not repair.

One morning, his granddaughter Nasreen asked her father, "Baba, how does Grandpa carry so much sadness? Doesn't it break him?"

Her father smiled, glancing at Yunis, whose lips still moved in the language of surrender. "He holds pain the way the Prophet ﷺ did. With faith that doesn't need to shout. He once told me that when your heart aches for what you cannot mend, whisper this dhikr."

> Hasbi Allahu
> La ilaha illa Huwa
> Alayhi tawakkaltu
> Wa Anta Rabbul-Arshil-Adheem

Oh Allah, You are enough for me, One and Eternal. I trust You to carry what I can't, to hold what hurts, and to take care of what I don't understand. You are the Lord of the Mighty Throne, and I leave this with You.

Later that day, Nasreen watched her grandfather. His fingers moved slowly along the prayer beads. Eyes closed. The dhikr fell like raindrops. Steady. Healing. Unseen.

Yunis didn't numb the pain. He entrusted it. Somehow, through surrender, he still believed in the possibility of mercy. For him, the dhikr wasn't a solution. It was a sacred posture. A way to keep hope alive, even when hope felt out of reach.

❋ · ❋ · ❋

Dear Friend,

The dhikr isn't about pretending everything is okay. It's about handing over the parts you cannot fix to the One who never fails.

So if you're tired, anxious, overwhelmed, or afraid, let this dhikr be your strength. Say the words slowly. Let your heart rest in the promise they carry. Let it become the breath that frees you, the whisper that holds you.

Let yourself be present.
Take a deep breath.
And begin:

> Hi God, it's me again. My thoughts feel tangled. My heart feels too full. I'm tired, anxious, overwhelmed, and maybe afraid. Please liberate me from sadness, depression, anxiety, fear, worry, pain, and hurt, and from the source of whatever is causing these feelings within me. I hand it all to You. I know You're enough for me. I know You'll take care of what I can't see and what I can't fix. I trust You. I need You. I surrender to You. I love You.

I submit to You, and I declare:

> Hasbi Allahu
> La ilaha illa Huwa
> Alayhi tawakkaltu
> Wa Anta Rabbul-Arshil-Adheem

> *Oh Allah, You are enough for me, One and Eternal. I trust You to carry what I can't, to hold what hurts, and to take care of what I don't understand. You are the Lord of the Mighty Throne, and I leave this with You.*

Chapter 7
When Prayer Breaks the Silence

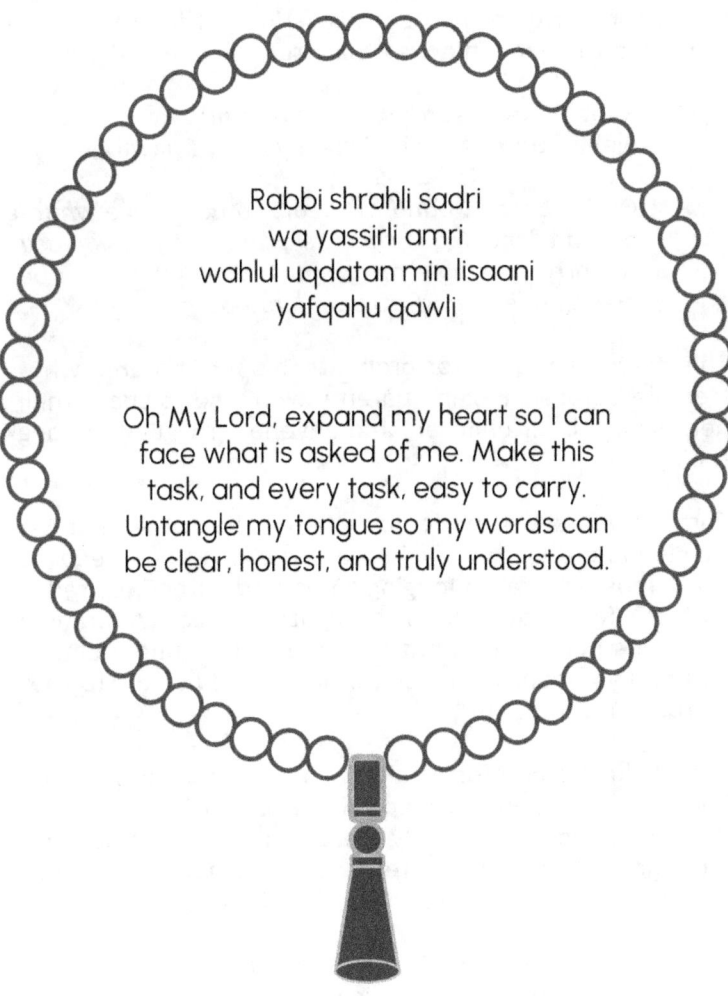

Rabbi shrahli sadri
wa yassirli amri
wahlul uqdatan min lisaani
yafqahu qawli

Oh My Lord, expand my heart so I can
face what is asked of me. Make this
task, and every task, easy to carry.
Untangle my tongue so my words can
be clear, honest, and truly understood.

Dear Friend

This dhikr reflects the prayer of Prophet Musa ﷺ when he was called to face Pharaoh and speak the truth. It is a prayer for clarity in the heart, ease in a difficult task, and the grace to speak in a way that truly reaches others.

> Rabbi shrahli sadri wa yassirli amri
> wahlul uqdatan min lisaani yafqahu qawli
>
> *Oh My Lord, expand my heart so I can face what is asked of me. Make this task, and every task, easy to carry. Untangle my tongue so my words can be clear, honest, and truly understood.*

This prayer isn't only for prophets. It's for students who tremble before an exam, parents who long to share their hearts with their children, and anyone struggling to speak their truth.

Perhaps you know the feeling. Words sit in your chest, tangled and unsure, refusing to come when you need them most. There's a longing to be understood, paired with the fear that your voice might not reach. A moment when the heart is full, but the mouth feels uncertain, and you find yourself hoping something sacred will help the words come through.

This dhikr is a comfort in those moments. Recite it when you face uncertainty. Whisper it before difficult conversations. Let it gently loosen the knots inside you, trusting that Allah, who created speech itself, can guide yours to reach the hearts of those who need it.

> Rabbi shrahli sadri wa yassirli amri
> wahlul uqdatan min lisaani yafqahu qawli
>
> *Oh My Lord, expand my heart so I can face what is asked of me. Make this task, and every task, easy to carry. Untangle my tongue so my words can be clear, honest, and truly understood.*

❀ The Healing Letter

Jamila hadn't spoken to her sister in five years. A rift over a family matter had deepened into years of silence. Words had failed her. They were either too harsh or not enough. One morning, she sat before a blank page, hoping to write the words that could heal.

She stared at the paper and began first began with:

Rabbi shrahli sadri wa yassirli amri
wahlul uqdatan min lisaani yafqahu qawli

Oh My Lord, expand my heart so I can face what is asked of me. Make this task, and every task, easy to carry. Untangle my tongue so my words can be clear, honest, and truly understood.

She wrote about childhood memories, the love they once shared, and the pain of separation. Her words poured out, not perfect but truthful. She left the letter at her sister's doorstep.

Days later, Jamila received a call. Tears and laughter followed. Healing began with a prayer that opened the door for an apology.

❀ The Exhale of Belief

Heather was nineteen when her questions began to shift.

She had grown up in a Catholic household filled with ritual and reverence. Sunday mornings at Mass, grace before meals, crosses on the walls. Then college opened a door. Through it came new voices and unfamiliar paths.

Heather found herself drawn to the calm sincerity of Muslim students on campus. She joined their circles, listened to their stories, and slowly became part of their gentle flow.

On Fridays, she entered the prayer room with light steps and an open heart. She didn't speak, but she listened. It was new to her.

She began to learn how to talk to God in a way she never had before. Not through ritual alone, but through presence. Through surrender.

Heather embraced Islam without ceremony. It was an inward shift, a gentle exhale of belief. She began to move through the world with new intention. Slowly. Naturally.

She struggled to tell her parents. They were kind, devout, proud of the faith they had passed down. Revealing that Islam had brought her a sense of completeness felt impossible. She feared the truth might wound them. All she wanted was to speak from the heart, without breaking theirs.

So she waited. She carried the silence gently. With it, this dhikr:

> Rabbi shrahli sadri wa yassirli amri
> wahlul uqdatan min lisaani yafqahu qawli
>
> *Oh My Lord, expand my heart so I can face what is asked of me. Make this task, and every task, easy to carry. Untangle my tongue so my words can be clear, honest, and truly understood.*

It became her anchor. Her courage. Her whispered prayer.

When she went home for the summer, they noticed a change. A peace that lingered. She whispered the dhikr in her heart, then spoke aloud what had long lived within her. She told them she had embraced Islam.

There was silence. A soft pause. They didn't understand. Not fully. Still, they saw the light in her eyes. The steadiness. The grace. In that moment, without needing all the answers, they embraced her. Not everything made sense. Her peace, though, did.

✸ The Unsent Message

Zayna didn't mean for it to go this far. It started with harmless replies. Friendly. Casual. Over time, the texting grew into something she couldn't ignore. She was drawn to Jaleel. His words made her feel seen. Deep down, she knew it wasn't right. Not for who she was. Not for the kind of love she prayed for.

She would sit with her phone, torn between reply and restraint. She began whispering this *dhikr* before reaching for her screen:

> Rabbi shrahli sadri wa yassirli amri
> wahlul uqdatan min lisaani yafqahu qawli
>
> *Oh My Lord, expand my heart so I can face what is asked of me. Make this task, and every task, easy to carry. Untangle my tongue so my words can be clear, honest, and truly understood.*

One evening, the words came. Not perfect. Sincere. "I don't think the way we're talking is helping either of us. It's not how I want to show up. Not for myself, and not for God."

She sent the message and put her phone down. Her hands shook. Her heart raced. Her soul felt lighter than it had in weeks.

Jaleel replied. A long pause. Then he said, "I've been struggling with this too. I just didn't know how to say it. I think you're right. It's time to end it."

Neither of them knew the other had been praying. Somehow, the prayers met. Without expectation. Without needing to be seen.

She found closure in the moment she chose God over impulse, in the prayer that opened her heart, steadied her voice, and gave her back her peace. Somehow, in that same surrender, Jaleel found peace too. Not from her words alone, but from the recognition that both of them had been praying for something more honest than desire.

Dear Friend,

Whether you are reaching out with trembling hands, turning inward with conviction, or letting go of a conversation you wish could have ended differently, this *dhikr* is for you. Let it guide you when your thoughts feel tangled and you're searching for clarity. Let it support you when your heart is tired but your intention is pure.

Let yourself be present.
Take a deep breath.
And begin:

> Hi God, it's me again. I'm trying to speak from the heart, but sometimes my words get tangled in fear, in longing, in doubt. Sometimes I don't know how to say what I mean. So please, expand my heart. Make this task, and every task, easy for me. Untangle my tongue. Help me speak what's true, even when it's tender. Let my words reflect what my heart holds. When I embrace silence, let that silence be my surrender. Let it be my trust that You will speak for me. Thank You, God. I trust You. I love You.

I submit to you and I declare:

> Rabbi shrahli sadri wa yassirli amri
> wahlul uqdatan min lisaani yafqahu qawli

> *Oh My Lord, expand my heart so I can face what is asked of me. Make this task, and every task, easy to carry. Untangle my tongue so my words can be clear, honest, and truly understood.*

Chapter 8
Between This World and the Next

Allahumma atina fi dunya hasanat
wa fil akhirati hasanat
wa qina 'adhaba annar

O God, give me what is good in this life.
Peace in my heart, purpose in my steps,
and love that lasts. Give me what is
good in the life to come. A home in
Your mercy, joy that endures, and
closeness to You. Keep me safe from
anything that distances me
from Your light.

Dear Friend,

This dhikr is one of the most encompassing and beloved supplications from the Quran. Its words are simple, but its meaning stretches wide. It is more than a request for comfort or ease. It is a declaration of trust in God's mercy. A yearning for balance. A plea for eternal safety.

> Allahumma atina fi dunya hasanat
> wa fil akhirati hasanat, wa qina 'adhaba annar
>
> *O God, give me what is good in this life. Peace in my heart, purpose in my steps, and love that lasts. Give me what is good in the life to come. A home in Your mercy, joy that endures, and closeness to You. Keep me safe from anything that distances me from Your light.*

It doesn't ask you to choose between the sacred and the worldly. It teaches that you can seek both. A meaningful life here and a blessed life beyond. This dhikr is for the anxious heart trying to make peace with the present and the unknown. It is for the one learning that goodness is not a luxury, but a grace. That protection is not just safety. It is salvation.

Whisper it when you feel torn between the pull of daily life and the call of the life to come. Say it when you long for beauty in your day and peace in your soul. It is your bridge between where you are and where you hope to be.

So let it rise again, from your heart to the heavens:

> Allahumma atina fi dunya hasanat
> wa fil akhirati hasanat, wa qina 'adhaba annar
>
> *O God, give me what is good in this life. Peace in my heart, purpose in my steps, and love that lasts. Give me what is good in the life to come. A home in Your mercy, joy that endures, and closeness to You. Keep me safe from anything that distances me from Your light.*

✿ Success, Rewritten

Nadia built her career with grit. Her days began early, stretched into late nights, and were driven by a steady push for perfection. She had what many called "success," but inside, she felt restless. Relationships faded. Prayer became occasional. Joy felt like a distant memory.

One afternoon, she found herself weeping. She didn't know why. It wasn't failure that broke her, but the absence of fulfillment. That night, she returned to her prayer mat and whispered:

> Allahumma atina fi dunya hasanat
> wa fil akhirati hasanat
> wa qina 'adhaba annar
>
> *O God, give me what is good in this life. Peace in my heart, purpose in my steps, and love that lasts. Give me what is good in the life to come. A home in Your mercy, joy that endures, and closeness to You. Keep me safe from anything that distances me from Your light.*

It wasn't a prayer for more accomplishments. It was a plea for peace. Slowly, she reconnected with her Creator, her community, and her heart. Her success didn't disappear. It now rested beside serenity.

She started attending a weekly halaqa, a small circle of learning and reflection, at a masjid tucked on the city's edge. The community there welcomed her not with judgment, but with gentle smiles. For the first time in years, Nadia lived not only as a professional, but as a seeker. Her heart softened. She discovered that healing often arrives not through answers, but through presence, and that true success is measured in closeness to the One who hears even whispered pleas.

❋ The Bees Knew Her Prayer

She moved slowly between the hives, her steps light, her breath steady. The mesh veil of her beekeeping suit fluttered with the breeze, but her hands remained still. Hadeel had learned this stillness from her mother, who had learned it from her grandfather. It was not just a craft. It was a trust.

The bees knew her. They circled her wrists, brushed past her shoulders, never in fear. She whispered the dhikr as she worked, voice low and familiar:

> Allahumma atina fi dunya hasanat
> wa fil akhirati hasanat
> wa qina 'adhaba annar
>
> *O God, give me what is good in this life. Peace in my heart, purpose in my steps, and love that lasts. Give me what is good in the life to come. A home in Your mercy, joy that endures, and closeness to You. Keep me safe from anything that distances me from Your light.*

Her mother used to say that bees could feel intention. That they honored gentleness. That they remembered kindness. Hadeel believed this. She had seen it. The way they moved with her, not against her. The way they waited when she paused. The way they stayed close, even when she was silent.

She lifted each frame with care, eyes scanning the honeycomb, heart steady. This was her offering. Not just the honey, but the way she gathered it gently, with prayer, with patience, with love.

She often thought of the Prophet Muhammad ﷺ, who spoke of mercy with every gesture, and whose words reminded her that gentleness is a form of worship.

She sealed each jar with gentleness, knowing the bees were looking at her. Before leaving the orchard, she stood still for a moment. Bees hovered near her, as if listening. She liked to believe they knew their offering was more than sweetness. It was *hasanat*, a goodness passed from wing to hand to heart.

She whispered once again:

> Allahumma atina fi dunya hasanat
> wa fil akhirati hasanat
> wa qina 'adhaba annar
>
> *O God, give me what is good in this life. Peace in my heart, purpose in my steps, and love that lasts. Give me what is good in the life to come. A home in Your mercy, joy that endures, and closeness to You. Keep me safe from anything that distances me from Your light.*

❀ Whispers Between Flames

Yusuf ran a small glass-blowing shop tucked into a place where life moved gently. The windows shimmered with color, and the shelves held lanterns, vases, and ornaments. Each one was shaped by heat, breath, and patience. He lived a humble life. His clothes were simple, his hands worn, his heart steady.

His son, Sabre, often joined him in the shop. He was young, yet already attuned to the flow of the craft. He watched the way his father moved with slow, deliberate gestures, never rushed. He learned how fragile glass could be, and how beauty sometimes came from what nearly broke.

They worked mostly in silence, guided by breath, fire, and a whispered prayer.

One evening, after the last lantern had cooled and the tools were set aside, Yusuf sat beside Sabre and said, "There's a prayer I've whispered for years. It's simple. It holds everything, somehow."

He recited:

> Allahumma atina fi dunya hasanat wa fil akhirati hasanat wa qina 'adhaba annar
>
> *O God, give me what is good in this life. Peace in my heart, purpose in my steps, and love that lasts. Give me what is good in the life to come. A home in Your mercy, joy that endures, and closeness to You. Keep me safe from anything that distances me from Your light.*

"It's a prayer for balance, for beauty in this life, and mercy in the next. I say it while shaping glass, when I'm tired, when I'm grateful. It reminds me that success isn't found in what we create, but in how close we stay to the One who gives breath and meaning."

Sabre listened quietly. He didn't respond right away. The next day, as he shaped a small vase, he whispered the prayer under his breath. It felt like prayer in motion. Like breath. Like flame

Years later, Sabre took over the shop. He taught others how to shape glass, how to move slowly, how to listen to silence. Sometimes, when the fire softened and the room held its breath, he would share the prayer his father had given him. Not as instruction, but as a companion. A way to ask for gentleness in this life, and light in the next.

Dear Friend,

This dhikr is one of the most balanced prayers we are taught. It speaks to our full journey. Life now, life later, and protection throughout. It reaches beyond comfort, asking for a life with purpose, a heart at rest, and an eternity held gently in mercy.

Goodness in this world might mean steady faith, kind company, or healing when things fall apart. In the Hereafter, it means closeness to the One who made you. In both, it begins with trust, the kind that allows goodness to unfold even when it cannot yet be seen.

Say it when you're unsure what to ask for. When words feel heavy and your heart needs rest. When you've given much, waited long, or simply need to remember what matters. Say it because it asks God to make this life meaningful, make the next life blessed, and keep you safe, always.

Let yourself be present.
Take a deep breath.
And begin:

> Hi God, it's me again. I feel tired from striving. At times, I feel lost. At times, I find myself chasing dreams, people, approval. I'm not sure what fills me anymore. I want to live a life that's beautiful not only in the eyes of the world, but in Yours. I ask You for goodness. Here in my every day, and in my forever. Protect me from pain that pulls me away from You. Let the path ahead be lit by Your wisdom. Keep me safe, keep me near.

I submit to You and declare:

Allahumma atina fi dunya hasanat wa fil akhirati hasanat wa qina 'adhaba annar

O God, give me what is good in this life. Peace in my heart, purpose in my steps, and love that lasts. Give me what is good in the life to come. A home in Your mercy, joy that endures, and closeness to You. Keep me safe from anything that distances me from Your light.

Chapter 9
My Heart in Your Hands

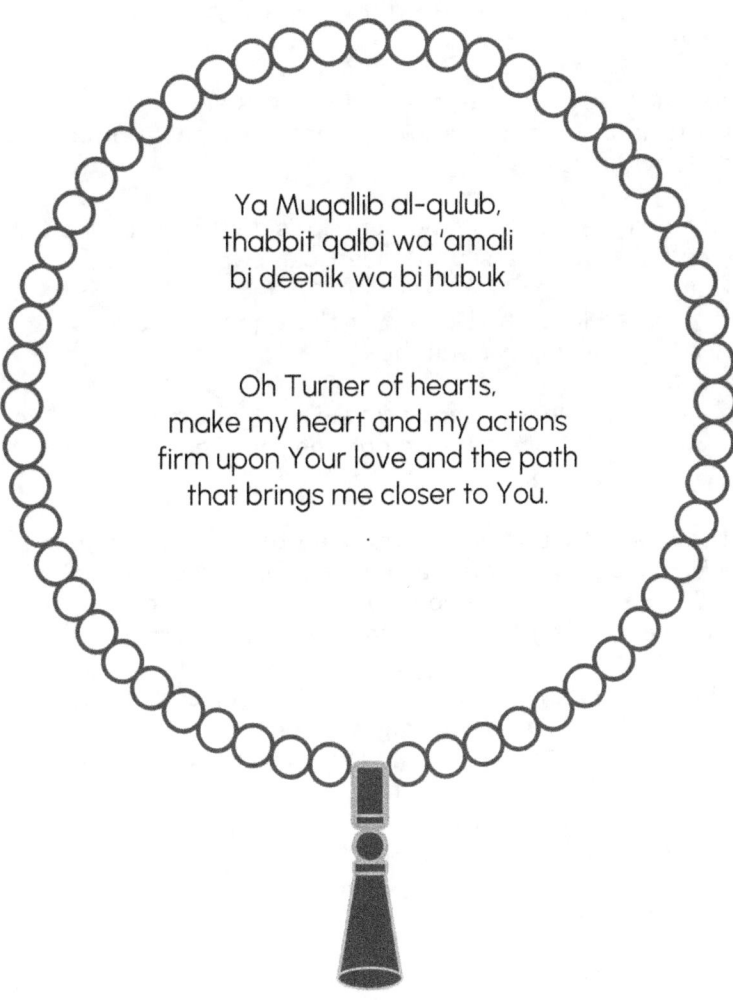

Ya Muqallib al-qulub,
thabbit qalbi wa 'amali
bi deenik wa bi hubuk

Oh Turner of hearts,
make my heart and my actions
firm upon Your love and the path
that brings me closer to You.

Dear Friend,

There are days when faith feels like a soft embrace. You feel held, guided, sure. Then there are days when it slips through your fingers, and you wonder if you're still being heard.

You may wake up with conviction and sleep with confusion. You may pray with tears one night and feel distant the next.

This dhikr is for those moments. It's a whisper to the One who knows how easily the heart can sway.

> Ya Muqallib al-qulub, thabbit qalbi wa 'amali
> bi deenik wa bi hubuk
>
> *Oh Turner of hearts, make my heart and my actions firm upon Your love and the path that brings me closer to You.*

The Prophet Muhammad ﷺ used to recite this often, even though his heart was already the purest. That alone tells us something. No one is immune to spiritual turbulence. No one is too strong to ask for stability.

This dhikr is not just a request. It is a surrender. It is saying, "God, I know I'm fragile. I know I forget. Still, I want to stay close to You. I want my love for You to be steady, and my actions to reflect that love."

Say it when you feel lost. Say it when you feel strong. Say it when you're unsure if your heart is drifting. Let it be your anchor.

> Ya Muqallib al-qulub, thabbit qalbi wa 'amali
> bi deenik wa bi hubuk
>
> *Oh Turner of hearts, make my heart and my actions firm upon Your love and the path that brings me closer to You.*

⦿ The Hijab of the Heart

Seham was a young adult, surrounded by girls she admired. They had already put on the hijab. Some with joy. Some with a calm strength. She watched them and felt both proud and unsettled.

She loved Allah. She prayed. She read the Quran like a letter from someone who knew her well. The hijab, though, felt like a step she wasn't ready for. Not because she didn't believe in it, but because something inside her still felt unsure.

She didn't tell anyone. Just kept nodding when friends talked about fabrics and pins. Smiled when people said, "Soon, insha'Allah." She wanted to be ready. She just wasn't.

One evening, after a long walk and a swirl of thoughts, she whispered:

> Ya Muqallib al-qulub, thabbit qalbi wa 'amali
> bi deenik wa bi hubuk
>
> *Oh Turner of hearts, make my heart and my actions firm upon Your love and the path that brings me closer to You.*

She began saying it every morning. Before school. Before family gatherings. Before looking in the mirror and wondering when.

It didn't rush her. It didn't shame her. It reminded her that love grows slowly, and Allah sees the heart before the cloth. He sees the spiritual hijab she's already wearing, woven with sincerity, stitched with longing, and softened by the colors of hope.

For Seham, the dhikr she returned to became her salvation. A way to stay near while still becoming. It reassured her that Allah was with her, and she would be ready when the time was right.

❂ The Breath Between Games

Adnan was seventeen and always moving. Between classes, basketball practice, group chats, and prayers whispered before sleep. He loved the game. The way it flowed. The way it made him feel strong and focused. Still, being a teenager felt like juggling too many selves at once.

He was rooted in faith. He loved Allah deeply. He tried to pray on time, to lower his gaze, to stay honest. Yet the world around him pulled in every direction. Some days, he felt like he was failing at everything. His deen, his friendships, even his own expectations.

He didn't talk about it much. Just kept showing up. Smiled at school. Played hard on the court. Made dua in the locker room when no one was looking.

One night, after missing maghrib and feeling guilty, he whispered:

> Ya Muqallib al-qulub, thabbit qalbi wa 'amali bi deenik wa bi hubuk
>
> *Oh Turner of hearts, make my heart and my actions firm upon Your love and the path that brings me closer to You.*

He started saying it before games. Before tests. Before walking into rooms where he felt unsure. It didn't fix everything, but it reminded him that he didn't have to carry it all alone.

For Adnan, the dhikr became a breath of steadiness. A way to stay close, even when life felt loud. It gave him something to return to, even when everything else kept changing.

❂ When Faith Holds What Feels Too Heavy

Jihad was twenty-two when something deep within them asked to be heard. It wasn't confusion or a passing thought. It was real, and it felt heavy.

They grew up close to faith, with a personal relationship with Allah. They joined youth circles and found peace in prayer, though this part of themselves felt too big to name .It stayed tucked inside. Tender, unspoken, and hard to carry. They didn't know how to be both whole and held. They feared that naming it might unravel the belonging they'd always known. So they carried it quietly, hoping God understood what they couldn't say out loud.

Jihad stayed silent. They didn't act on what they felt, but they lived with it. Cried during tahajjud. Prayed through the heaviness. Smiled when expected. Broke in silence, with sorrow never far.

One night, they whispered:

Ya Muqallib al-qulub, thabbit qalbi wa 'amali
bi deenik wa bi hubuk

Oh Turner of hearts, make my heart and my actions firm upon Your love and the path that brings me closer to You.

They began reciting the dhikr daily. It didn't erase their feelings, yet it offered clarity. One day, they wrote in their journal, "I may never be understood by everyone, but what I do know is that I love God, and He loves me. And for that love, I will never let Him go."

For Jihad, the dhikr wasn't a cure. It was a companion. A reminder that even in the most personal struggles, the heart can still choose love, faith, and surrender.

Dear Friend

Your heart is a traveler. It moves through seasons, emotions, doubts, and dreams. This dhikr is your compass. It doesn't promise that you'll never feel lost. It promises you'll always have a way back.

Recite it when your faith feels fragile, when your love for Allah feels distant, when you want your actions to match your intentions. Let it be your way of staying near, even when certainty feels far.

Say it when the masks feel heavy, when you're ready to speak from the soul, when your heart needs a place to land.

Let yourself be present.
Take a deep breath.
And begin:

> Hi God, it's me again. My heart feels unsettled. I want to love You with presence, not just in moments of need. I want my actions to reflect devotion, not just habit. Please hold my heart close, guide my steps, and help me grow with gentleness. Remind me that You see the longing before the action, and the heart before the words. Please make me firm in Your love and Your path.

I submit to You and I declare:

> Ya Muqallib al-qulub, thabbit qalbi wa 'amali bi deenik wa bi hubuk
>
> *Oh Turner of hearts, make my heart and my actions firm upon Your love and the path that brings me closer to You.*

Chapter 10
The Home of my Regret and Reliance

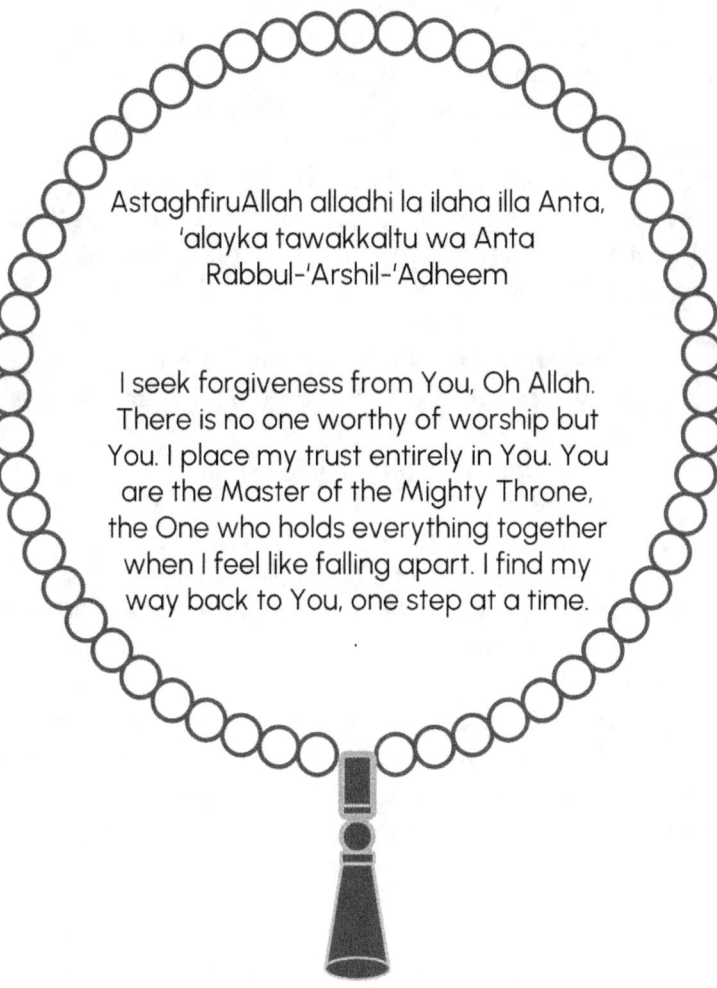

AstaghfiruAllah alladhi la ilaha illa Anta, 'alayka tawakkaltu wa Anta Rabbul-'Arshil-'Adheem

I seek forgiveness from You, Oh Allah. There is no one worthy of worship but You. I place my trust entirely in You. You are the Master of the Mighty Throne, the One who holds everything together when I feel like falling apart. I find my way back to You, one step at a time.

Dear Friend,

There are moments when regret feels near. Not loud, but lasting. Not sharp, but heavy. You may carry the weight of choices you wish you hadn't made. Words you wish you hadn't said. Paths you wish you hadn't walked. In those moments, this dhikr becomes a lifeline.

It's not only a plea for forgiveness. It's a humble declaration of surrender. It says I've made mistakes, but I still believe. I've stumbled, but I still trust. I've been weak, but I know You are strong.

> AstaghfiruAllah alladhi la ilaha illa Anta,
> 'alayka tawakkaltu wa Anta Rabbul-'Arshil-'Adheem

> *I seek forgiveness from You, Oh Allah. There is no one worthy of worship but You. I place my trust entirely in You. You are the Master of the Mighty Throne, the One who holds everything together when I feel like falling apart. I find my way back to You, one step at a time.*

This dhikr is for the one who wants to come back. The one who feels distant, or even disconnected. The one who wonders if it's too late but still hopes it isn't. The one who trusts that Allah's mercy is greater than their missteps.

Say it when guilt whispers too loudly. When the past plays on repeat and you wonder if you'll ever feel free again. Say it when you want to begin again, even if you're not sure how. Say it when you're ready to stop carrying what was never yours to hold alone. The shame. The silence. The stories you've told yourself about being unworthy. Say it because you are not alone. Say it because Allah hears you. Say it because mercy was always meant for moments like this.

AstaghfiruAllah alladhi la ilaha illa Anta,
'alayka tawakkaltu wa Anta Rabbul-'Arshil-'Adheem

I seek forgiveness from You, Oh Allah. There is no one worthy of worship but You. I place my trust entirely in You. You are the Master of the Mighty Throne, the One who holds everything together when I feel like falling apart. I find my way back to You, one step at a time.

✿ When We Drift, God Stays

Sami wasn't the most religious person growing up. He didn't lead prayers or give reminders during Ramadan. Faith was still present, resting in the background. There were childhood memories of praying beside his parents, a Quran tucked on the shelf, and a sense of comfort whenever they heard the adhan.

College changed things. New friends. New habits. Late nights. Missed prayers. It wasn't rebellion. It was slow drifting. A downward unraveling. Sami didn't reject faith. He just stopped reaching for it.

At first, he didn't notice. One missed Fajr turned into two. Friday prayers became optional. The Quran app stayed unopened. They told themselves they were just busy. Just tired. Just adjusting.

One night, after a party, Sami sat alone in their dorm room. The music still echoed in the hallway, yet inside, there was silence. A kind of emptiness that no playlist could fill.

Late that night, Sami opened his phone. Among the notifications and unread texts was a message from an old friend. It had been sent months ago, but now it felt full of meaning. "Salaam Sami, it's been a while. I just wanted you to know that when we drift, God stays. He hears our return, and waits patiently for the step toward Him. Remember this dhikr:

> AstaghfiruAllah alladhi la ilaha illa Anta,
> 'alayka tawakkaltu wa Anta Rabbul-'Arshil-'Adheem
>
> *I seek forgiveness from You, Oh Allah. There is no one worthy of worship but You. I place my trust entirely in You. You are the Master of the Mighty Throne, the One who holds everything together when I feel like falling apart. I find my way back to You, one step at a time.*

Sami whispered it. Once. Then again. Then again. Tears followed. Not from shame, but from longing. Longing to feel close again. Longing to feel clean again.

He began praying again. Quietly. Imperfectly. Consistently. He didn't announce it. He didn't post about it. He just returned. For Sami, dhikr was a way back to peace.

✸ The One Who Hid Their Pain

Noor was always smiling. Always helping. Always saying "Alhamdulillah," even when things were hard. Beneath it all, they carried a hidden secret, a silent burden. A choice they deeply regretted. One that remained unspoken. One that lingered.

It wasn't a public mistake. Nothing anyone would suspect. It lived inside them like a soft shadow. They feared judgment. They feared being unworthy. They feared that one moment had unraveled everything.

They stopped praying regularly. Not out of defiance, but out of shame. They felt undeserving of standing before Allah.

One night, after a long cry, Noor remembered a friend's voice. They had once said, "Say this when you feel broken:

AstaghfiruAllah alladhi la ilaha illa Anta,
'alayka tawakkaltu wa Anta Rabbul-'Arshil-'Adheem

I seek forgiveness from You, Oh Allah. There is no one worthy of worship but You. I place my trust entirely in You. You are the Master of the Mighty Throne, the One who holds everything together when I feel like falling apart. I find my way back to You, one step at a time.

Noor whispered it. Not once, but again and again. It became a gentle anchor. A way to feel held. A reminder that Allah sees the heart, not just the history.

They began journaling. Praying. Slowly forgiving themselves. They didn't tell anyone. They told God. That was enough.

The shame softened into strength. The past hadn't disappeared. It was simply no longer the measure of their worth.

For Noor, this dhikr wasn't about being perfect. It was about being honest. That honesty became healing, and with it came a steady return to God.

⚙ When Asking Faded

Jumana used to ask God for everything. Guidance. Protection. Ease. Even small things, like finding her keys or calming her heart before a meeting. The asking didn't disappear all at once. It faded slowly, almost without her realizing. She just stopped reaching out as often. Life kept moving, and her prayers slipped into the background.

She still said "Alhamdulillah." Still smiled. Still helped others. Inside, though, something felt distant.

One afternoon, Jumana went for a walk in the park. She overheard a conversation between a young girl and her grandmother. Though soft, something about it stayed with her. The young girl asked, "Tata, do you think there are trees in heaven with leaves like roses?"

Jumana didn't interrupt. She listened. That conversation gave her space to reflect

That evening, she sat alone and whispered a dhikr she hadn't said in years:

> AstaghfiruAllah alladhi la ilaha illa Anta,
> 'alayka tawakkaltu wa Anta Rabbul-'Arshil-'Adheem
>
> *I seek forgiveness from You, Oh Allah. There is no one worthy of worship but You. I place my trust entirely in You. You are the Master of the Mighty Throne, the One who holds everything together when I feel like falling apart. I find my way back to You, one step at a time.*

She didn't ask for anything. She just said it. Slowly. Softly. Like a breath returning to its source.

The next morning, she whispered it again. Then again the day after. Not out of habit, but out of longing. Not to be answered, but to be held.

The words didn't fix everything. Still, they opened something. A door she hadn't realized she'd closed.

Jumana began speaking to God again. First with presence.
Then with truth. Slowly, with requests.

❋ · ❋ · ❋

Dear Friend,

You are not your worst moment. You are not your biggest
mistake. You are a soul still capable of light, still worthy
of love, still invited into mercy.

This dhikr is your return ticket. Your honest confession.
Your bold surrender. Your unspoken truth. It waits without
judgment. Without an expiration date.

Say it when you feel heavy. Say it when you feel hopeful.
Say it when you want to trust again. Say it when you're
tired of pretending. When you want to be real with God.
When you're ready for your heart to stop hiding and start
healing.

Let yourself be present.
Take a deep breath.
And begin:

> Hi God, it's me again. I've made mistakes. I've
> carried guilt. I've tried to fix things on my own. I've
> run from You when I felt unworthy, hidden when I
> should have reached out. I've doubted Your mercy,
> even while longing for it. Now I come to You. Not
> with perfect words. Just with a tired heart. I seek
> Your forgiveness. I place my trust in You. You are
> the Lord of the Majestic Throne. I am in front of
> Your door. It's open. I walk in, trusting You'll
> receive me, just as I am.

I submit to You and I declare:

AstaghfiruAllah alladhi la ilaha illa Anta,
'alayka tawakkaltu wa Anta
Rabbul-'Arshil-'Adheem

*I seek forgiveness from You, Oh Allah. There is no
one worthy of worship but You. I place my trust
entirely in You. You are the Master of the Mighty
Throne, the One who holds everything together
when I feel like falling apart. I find my way back to
You, one step at a time.*

Chapter 11
By His Name, I Begin and Trust

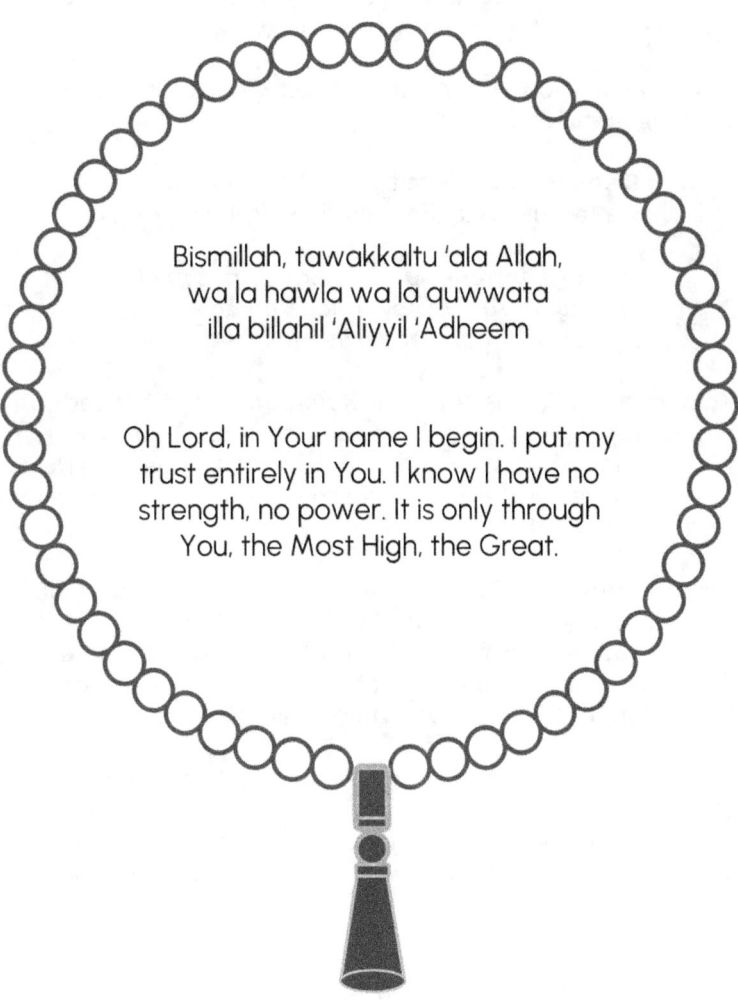

Bismillah, tawakkaltu 'ala Allah,
wa la hawla wa la quwwata
illa billahil 'Aliyyil 'Adheem

Oh Lord, in Your name I begin. I put my
trust entirely in You. I know I have no
strength, no power. It is only through
You, the Most High, the Great.

Dear Friend.

This dhikr is for the moments when you're about to step into something uncertain. When your heart is racing. When your mind feels clouded with doubt. When you whisper, "I don't know how this will work out."

It's a declaration. A surrender. A reminder that you are not walking alone.

> Bismillah, tawakkaltu 'ala Allah, wa la hawla wa la quwwata illa billahil 'Aliyyil 'Adheem
>
> *Oh Lord, in Your name I begin. I put my trust entirely in You. I know I have no strength, no power. It is only through You, the Most High, the Great.*

This is the dhikr the Prophet Muhammad ﷺ recited when stepping into the unknown. It's more than words. It's a legacy of trust. A soft echo that faith doesn't erase fear, but gives you the courage to walk forward, knowing God is already there.

Say it before a difficult conversation. Say it before a job interview. Say it when you're waiting for test results, or trying to hold your family together. Say it when you're standing at the edge of something new, and you need to believe that God is already there, making a way.

This dhikr is a doorway to miracles. Not because it changes the world around you instantly, but because it changes the way you walk through it. It reminds you that your strength is not your own. It belongs to God. When you trust Him, you're not walking into the unknown. You are walking into His care.

> Bismillah, tawakkaltu 'ala Allah, wa la hawla wa la quwwata illa billahil 'Aliyyil 'Adheem
>
> *Oh Lord, in Your name I begin. I put my trust entirely in You. I know I have no strength, no power. It is only through You, the Most High, the Great.*

⚙ The Mothers Drive

Samira was exhausted. Her son had been sick for weeks, and the doctors still couldn't find the cause. She had taken time off work, drained her savings, and spent countless nights praying beside his bed. Her heart was heavy with fear, and her body was worn from worry.

Now she was driving him to yet another hospital. The silence in the car felt thick. Her hands trembled on the steering wheel.

She whispered the dhikr aloud:

> Bismillah, tawakkaltu 'ala Allah, wa la hawla wa la quwwata illa billahil 'Aliyyil 'Adheem
>
> *Oh Lord, in Your name I begin. I put my trust entirely in You. I know I have no strength, no power. It is only through You, the Most High, the Great.*

Her son looked up from the back seat. "Mama, what does that mean?" "It means," she said softly, "I'm not driving alone."

At the hospital, the doctors finally found the cause. It was treatable. Her son would recover. Relief flooded her chest. Even more than relief, she felt awe.

She had walked into that day with nothing but prayer. That had been enough.

For Samira, the miracle wasn't just healing. It was the strength to keep going when she had nothing left but faith. It was the reminder that even in her weakest moments, God was guiding the wheel.

❋ Trust Was Her First Step

Sundus sat on the edge of her bed, staring at the suitcase she had just zipped shut. Her marriage was ending. The papers were signed. Now she was preparing to leave the home she had helped build.

What hurt most wasn't the divorce. It was leaving behind her stepdaughter, Marwa.

They had grown close over the years. Sundus had braided her hair, helped with homework, whispered prayers over her when she was sick. They baked cookies on rainy afternoons, crafted handmade cards for Eid. Marwa had called her "Mama Sundus," and now, Sundus didn't know how to explain this goodbye. It felt like leaving behind a part of her own heart.

At the door, she paused. Then whispered:

> Bismillah, tawakkaltu 'ala Allah, wa la hawla wa la quwwata illa billahil 'Aliyyil 'Adheem
>
> *Oh Lord, in Your name I begin. I put my trust entirely in You. I know I have no strength, no power. It is only through You, the Most High, the Great.*

She didn't know what the future held. What she did know was that God would carry her through the grief and the unknown.

Years passed. Sundus adjusted to a life that felt different, but still held meaning. She prayed for Marwa every night.

Then one afternoon, a message arrived: *"Hi Mama Sundus. I found your blog. I miss you. Can we talk?"*

They met at a café where time seemed to slow. Marwa was older now, but her eyes were the same. They talked. They laughed. They began again, not from the beginning, but from where they were.

For Sundus, the miracle wasn't just reconnection. It was the assurance that when you trust God through heartbreak, He writes chapters you never thought to ask for.

❀ We Work. He Heals

Dr. Ibrahim adjusted his gloves. It wasn't the dental work that made him pause. It was what patients carried inside. A migraine that felt like a toothache. Sadness tucked behind a smile. Fear hidden in the ordinary.

His childhood friend, Dr. Latif, stood quietly beside him. They had played basketball together as boys, kept each other anchored throughout college, and now ran a dental clinic that felt less like a business and more like a prayer.

Patients often said there was something different about the space. Something unspoken. Before every procedure, whether routine or rare, the two dentists would pause and whisper the dhikr:

Bismillah, tawakkaltu 'ala Allah, wa la hawla wa la quwwata illa billahil 'Aliyyil 'Adheem

Oh Lord, in Your name I begin. I put my trust entirely in You. I know I have no strength, no power. It is only through You, the Most High, the Great.

They didn't recite it out of habit. They recited it because they knew that no degree, no steady hand, no advanced tool could bring healing without His permission.

Some patients cried before anything started. Others held their breath. A few shared stories they'd never told. Through it all, the dhikr flowed gently from Dr. Latif and Dr. Ibrahim. It steadied the room. It met fear with kindness. It lingered in the air. It softened the light.

One evening, after closing, Dr. Latif looked up from his paperwork and said, "It feels like every appointment is an act of surrender." Dr. Ibrahim nodded. "We work. He heals."

❀ · ❀ · ❀

Dear Friend,

This dhikr is your anchor in uncertainty. It is your shield in fear. It is your reminder that you are never walking alone.

Say it when you're scared. Say it when you're unsure. Say it when you're about to do something brave. Say it when you're on the edge of completing something and you know, deep in your heart, that it can only be done with His supervision. Say it when you don't know what else to say.

Let yourself be present.
Take a deep breath.
And begin:

> Hi God, it's me again. I'm about to step into something I can't control. I feel scared. I feel unsure, but I trust You. I trust Your wisdom. I trust Your timing. I trust that You are with me, even when I feel alone. I don't know what will happen next, but I know You see the whole picture. So I'll take the next step, holding onto You.

I submit to You and I declare:

> Bismillah, tawakkaltu 'ala Allah, wa la hawla wa la quwwata illa billahil 'Aliyyil 'Adheem

> *Oh Lord, in Your name I begin. I put my trust entirely in You. I know I have no strength, no power. It is only through You, the Most High, the Great.*

Chapter 12
You Are Enough for Me

La ilaha illAllah,
wahdahu la sharika lah
Lahul-mulk wa lahul-hamd,
wa huwa 'ala kulli shay'in qadeer

There is no one I turn to but You.
No one shares in Your being, Your
mercy, or Your power. All that exists
belongs to You. Every praise that rises
from my heart is Yours. You are able to
do all things. I have nothing unless You
choose to give.

Dear Friend,

This dhikr is the heartbeat of faith. It is the grounding truth we carry through joy and hardship. God is One. There is none who holds His mercy, His presence, or His strength. Everything we experience, from every tear to every triumph to every breath, is held in His care. All that exists belongs to Him. He is able to do all things.

> La ilaha illAllah, wahdahu la sharika lah
> Lahul-mulk wa lahul-hamd,
> wa huwa 'ala kulli shay'in qadeer

> *There is no one I turn to but You. No one shares in Your being, Your mercy, or Your power. All that exists belongs to You. Every praise that rises from my heart is Yours. You are able to do all things. I have nothing unless You choose to give.*

Say it when you feel overwhelmed, when you need to remember who holds the keys to the unseen. Say it when life feels out of control and you need to anchor yourself in the One who is in control. Say it when happiness fills your heart, when blessings are easy to name and gratitude flows without effort.

This is the dhikr of surrender. The dhikr of awe. The dhikr that realigns you with the truth. As the Prophet Muhammad ﷺ taught us, nothing is too broken, too far gone, or too complicated for God to heal, guide, or transform. Trust that every whisper reaches Him. He is not just able. He is always able.

> La ilaha illAllah, wahdahu la sharika lah.
> Lahul-mulk wa lahul-hamd,
> wa huwa 'ala kulli shay'in qadeer

> *There is no one I turn to but You. No one shares in Your being, Your mercy, or Your power. All that exists belongs to You. Every praise that rises from my heart is Yours. You are able to do all things. I have nothing unless You choose to give.*

⚙ The Jeweler's Secret

In a tucked-away corner of the marketplace, Nasir worked patiently, shaping beauty with hands trained by time. His son, Mohsin, sat beside him, learning the delicate art of melting gold, setting gems, and polishing metal until it glowed.

Every evening, as they polished jewelry, Mohsin noticed something curious. His father's lips always moved silently, as if whispering to someone unseen.

One day, curiosity overcame hesitation. "Dad," Mohsin asked gently, "why do your lips move while you work?"

His father smiled and replied, "As gold needs polishing to shine, so does the heart. While I work, I remember God. He gently whispered:

> La ilaha illAllah, wahdahu la sharika lah.
> Lahul-mulk wa lahul-hamd,
> wa huwa 'ala kulli shay'in qadeer
>
> *There is no one I turn to but You. No one shares in Your being, Your mercy, or Your power. All that exists belongs to You. Every praise that rises from my heart is Yours. You are able to do all things. I have nothing unless You choose to give.*

"These words polish more than ornaments. They cleanse sorrow, pride, and distraction. They remind me that everything belongs to Him."

From that day on, father and son polished jewelry side by side. Hands busy. Hearts anchored. Lips moving in soft remembrance.

❁ The Back Row

Haroon had lived a complicated life. His twenties were messy. Choices made in haste, love traded for distraction, years blurred by regret. Now in his forties, he sat in the back row of a mosque, unsure if he belonged.

The etiquette was unfamiliar. The verses, forgotten. Yet one phrase from his childhood remained:

> La ilaha illAllah, wahdahu la sharika lah.
> Lahul-mulk wa lahul-hamd,
> wa huwa 'ala kulli shay'in qadeer
>
> *There is no one I turn to but You. No one shares in Your being, Your mercy, or Your power. All that exists belongs to You. Every praise that rises from my heart is Yours. You are able to do all things. I have nothing unless You choose to give.*

He whispered it quietly, almost shyly. Not to be heard. Not to be seen. Just to return.

Something shifted inside him. It wasn't dramatic. It was honest. A moment where the distance between him and God felt less impossible.

He realized this dhikr wasn't asking for perfection. It was offering forgiveness. It wasn't demanding eloquence. It was inviting return.

✿ In Her Arms, In His Mercy

Aya held her newborn son in the hush of an early morning. The room was dim, the silence broken only by his small breaths against her chest. Feedings. Diapers. The slow unraveling of sleep. Everything felt new and heavy. Her husband had grown silent again. The space between them stretched thin. She hadn't said it aloud, but the thought lingered. She was doing this alone.

The baby nestled closer, and Aya began to rock gently. A dhikr came to her, one her grandmother used to whisper while folding laundry, cooking, praying.

> La ilaha illAllah, wahdahu la sharika lah.
> Lahul-mulk wa lahul-hamd,
> wa huwa 'ala kulli shay'in qadeer

> *There is no one I turn to but You. No one shares in Your being, Your mercy, or Your power. All that exists belongs to You. Every praise that rises from my heart is Yours. You are able to do all things. I have nothing unless You choose to give.*

She repeated it, like a lullaby.

She didn't feel stronger, but she felt steadier. Like she was no longer raising her son alone. Like she was part of something timeless.

For Aya, this dhikr wasn't a routine. It was a whisper of trust, breathing through motherhood. Each breath, a reminder that God was with her and her baby. Not distant. Not abstract. But near, like a Friend who listened before she spoke, and knew what her heart was carrying. In the sincere repetition of this dhikr, she felt held. Protected. Accompanied.

Dear Friend,

This dhikr is a re-centering. It gathers the scattered pieces of your heart and returns them to the One who never left. It reminds you that God sees you in the quiet moments, the uncertain ones, the ones where love feels distant or strength feels thin. He sees what others overlook. He knows the weight you carry, the silence you keep, the prayers you whisper from the back row. His mercy is not far, but near enough to steady your breath and remind you that your worth was never hidden from Him.

Say it when you feel small. Say it when courage feels distant. Say it when you want to remember that nothing can separate you from the One who is able. Not your fears. Not your past. Not your questions. Say it when you are thankful. When you smile after a long journey. When you feel loved, seen, and blessed. Say it then, too.

Let yourself be present.
Take a deep breath.
And begin:

> Hi God, it's me again. You own all things. You deserve all praise. I believe, with all the broken pieces of me, that You have power over everything. Over my fears. Over my hopes. Over the things I can't name but feel deeply. I trust that You are near. I love You.

I submit to You and I declare:

> La ilaha illAllah, wahdahu la sharika lah.
> Lahul-mulk wa lahul-hamd,
> wa huwa 'ala kulli shay'in qadeer

> *There is no one I turn to but You. No one shares in Your being, Your mercy, or Your power. All that exists belongs to You. Every praise that rises from my heart is Yours. You are able to do all things. I have nothing unless You choose to give.*

Chapter 13
What Words Cannot Hold

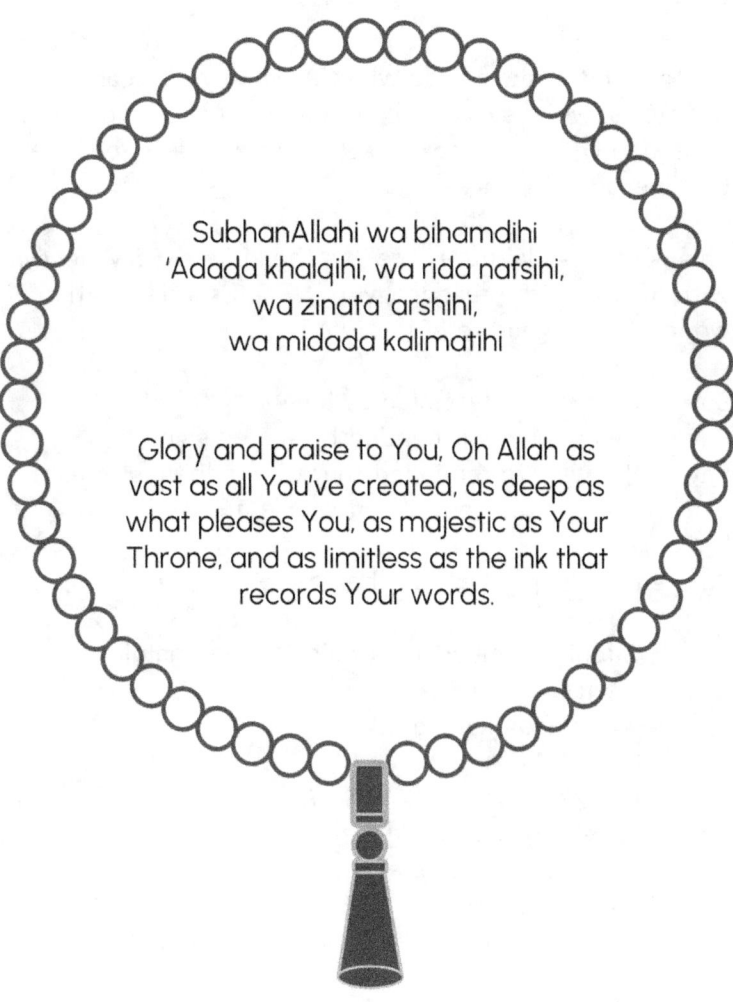

SubhanAllahi wa bihamdihi
'Adada khalqihi, wa rida nafsihi,
wa zinata 'arshihi,
wa midada kalimatihi

Glory and praise to You, Oh Allah as
vast as all You've created, as deep as
what pleases You, as majestic as Your
Throne, and as limitless as the ink that
records Your words.

Dear Friend,

Some praises are gentle. Some are grand. This dhikr is both.

It's the kind of praise you whisper when your heart overflows, when everything around you feels tender and alive, and when your soul reaches for a "thank You" that lives beyond language.

This isn't a casual utterance. It's the kind you say slowly, with breath, with presence, with awe. It's a declaration of wonder and a gesture of gratitude.

Say it when you're humbled by love.
Say it when you're surrounded by sacred signs.
Say it when you're reminded that God didn't just create beauty. He created your ability to see it.

So breathe deeply. Let your heart expand. Then whisper:

> SubhanAllahi wa bihamdihi 'Adada khalqihi,
> wa rida nafsihi, wa zinata 'arshihi,
> wa midada kalimatihi
>
> *Glory and praise to You, Oh Allah*
> *as vast as all You've created,*
> *as deep as what pleases You,*
> *as majestic as Your Throne,*
> *and as limitless as the ink that records Your words*

❁ The Doctor's Pause

Dr. Ansari had spent over a decade in family medicine. She had seen newborns take their first breaths and elders take their last. She had given good news, difficult news, and sometimes no answers at all.

Between patients, there was a small habit. A pause. A whisper.

> SubhanAllahi wa bihamdihi 'Adada khalqihi,
> wa rida nafsihi, wa zinata 'arshihi,
> wa midada kalimatihi
>
> *Glory and praise to You, Allah,*
> *as vast as all You've created,*
> *as deep as what pleases You,*
> *as majestic as Your Throne,*
> *and as limitless as the ink that records Your words*

No one saw it. No one needed to.

Dr. Ansari didn't quote religious texts during appointments. She didn't speak about faith in the exam room. Each time she felt unsure, each time she sensed a patient's pain, this dhikr rose quietly. It wasn't meant to be noticed. It was there to hold her steady.

It reminded her that she was not the healer. God was. It reminded her that compassion had weight. That presence mattered.

One day, after a check-up, an elderly patient placed a hand on Dr. Ansari's arm and said, "You make me feel safe." For Dr. Ansari, that was the miracle. Not curing every illness, but offering dignity.

And each time she whispered the dhikr again, it felt like placing that praise into the hands of the One who knows every heart.

❁ The Stargazer's Transformation

Adam was seventeen and drawn to the sky. Not the dreamy kind, but the kind filled with data and diagrams.

He loved tracking constellations, staying up late with a telescope and messy notebooks. Still, there were nights when science didn't feel like enough. He wanted to believe that behind all the patterns, something was listening.

On nights when the moon felt like a secret and the stars held their breath, Adam would whisper:

> SubhanAllahi wa bihamdihi 'Adada khalqihi,
> wa rida nafsihi, wa zinata 'arshihi,
> wa midada kalimatihi
>
> *Glory and praise to You, Allah,*
> *as vast as all You've created,*
> *as deep as what pleases You,*
> *as majestic as Your Throne,*
> *and as limitless as the ink that records Your words*

He didn't say it to impress. He said it because awe needed a voice. Looking at galaxies billions of light-years away, he felt something strange. Not small, but seen. As if the One who created those stars also knew every pulse in his chest.

What began as routine became revelation. The dhikr softened him. It taught him to pause, to feel, to marvel. Not just at stars, but at the One who placed them there.

For Adam, the miracle wasn't reaching the stars. It was waking up to the One who placed them there.

❋ The Grandmothers Prayer

Each morning after Fajr, Lam'a, whom the neighbors respectfully called Um Salih, stepped into her sacred courtyard. The breeze still carried traces of night. The world was still tucked in. One thing, though, had always awakened early. The morning call to prayer drifted through the air with the subtle scent of her jasmine tree.

It stood tall against the stone wall, fragrant and familiar. She greeted it like an old friend. On the mornings when her granddaughter Cima was present, Lam'a's eyes would brighten as she recited with a smile, "Sabah al-full wa al-yasmin wa al-zanbaq. Wa lighayrik ma biyilbaq. *A morning of jasmine, lilies, and grace, and for no one but you does it suit so perfectly.*"

She poured water at its roots, whispered a few blessings, and settled into her wooden chair beneath its shade. In one hand, her tasbih. In the other, a small cup of jasmine tea. Warm, floral, comforting.

Then came the dhikr:

> SubhanAllahi wa bihamdihi 'Adada khalqihi,
> wa rida nafsihi, wa zinata 'arshihi,
> wa midada kalimatihi
>
> *Glory and praise to You, Allah,*
> *as vast as all You've created,*
> *as deep as what pleases You,*
> *as majestic as Your Throne,*
> *and as limitless as the ink that records Your words*

One hundred times. For her children. Her grandchildren. For the ones she hadn't seen in years but still felt close to.

Sometimes, she'd pause and name them between beads. "Ya Allah, for Salih's wisdom. For Cima's gentleness. For Dima's steadiness. For Ibtisam's light. For Issam's protection. For Omar's clarity. For Oliver's joy. For Huda's peace."

For Tata Lam'a, it was through her daily dhikr that she found closeness with Allah, and in that closeness, a tender safeguard formed around her and her lineage.

✸ · ✸ · ✸

Dear Friend,

This dhikr is your sunrise. Your telescope. Your breath between appointments. It's your way of saying, "God, I see You in everything, and I praise You for it all." It's that heartbeat of stillness when the world feels like it's holding its breath.

Say it when beauty overwhelms you.
Say it when love stretches your heart.
Say it when silence invites reflection.
Say it when the fragrance of nature reminds you that something sacred is always near.

Let yourself be present.
Take a deep breath.
And begin:

> Hi God, it's me again. I feel the wonder. I see the signs. I don't have all the words, but You've given me this one, and it carries more than I can say. I speak it in moments I understand, and in the ones I don't. For the beauty that moves me, and the silence that steadies me. For the people I love, and the ones I'm still learning to love. For the questions I carry, and the peace I'm learning to trust.

I submit to You and I declare:

> SubhanAllahi wa bihamdihi 'Adada khalqihi,
> wa rida nafsihi, wa zinata 'arshihi,
> wa midada kalimatihi
>
> *Glory and praise to You, Allah,*
> *as vast as all You've created,*
> *as deep as what pleases You,*
> *as majestic as Your Throne,*
> *and as limitless as the ink that records Your words*

Chapter 14
Not Even for a Blink

Ya Hayyu Ya Qayyum,
birahmatika astagheeth,
aslih li sha'ni kullahu, wa la takilni ila
nafsi wa la ila ahadin min khalqeka
tarfata 'ayn.

Oh Lord, You are the Ever-Living, the
One who sustains everything. I'm
leaning on Your mercy. Please help me.
Make things right in every part of my
life, and don't leave me to myself or to
anyone from Your creation,
not even for a blink.

Dear Friend,

This dhikr is for the days that feel heavy. When your to-do list is long but your energy is short. When your heart is racing but your mind can't catch up. When the silence feels loud and the pressure to be okay becomes unbearable. It's for the moments when you realize you cannot hold everything together. Perhaps you were never meant to carry it all alone.

This dhikr isn't just a call for help. It's an invitation to surrender. It's the whispered prayer of someone who's tired of pretending they're fine. It's the soul's way of saying, "God, I need You. I cannot do this alone."

Just as the Prophet Muhammad ﷺ turned to God in his moments of weariness, we too can let this dhikr become our peaceful turning.

> Ya Hayyu Ya Qayyum, birahmatika astagheeth,
> aslih li sha'ni kullahu, wa la takilni ila nafsi
> wa la ila ahadin min khalqeka tarfata 'ayn.
>
> *Oh Lord, You are the Ever-Living, the One who*
> *sustains everything. I'm leaning on Your mercy.*
> *Please help me. Make things right in every part of*
> *my life, and don't leave me to myself or to anyone*
> *from Your creation, not even for a blink.*

Say it when you're standing at the edge of exhaustion. Say it when you don't know the answer, but you know the One who holds them. Say it when you want to ask for help without explaining everything.

✸ When the Calendar Cleared

Tasnim was a community organizer. Brilliant, passionate, relentless. Her calendar was a blur of meetings, rallies, and late-night strategy calls. She cared deeply. She worked tirelessly.

She also has ADHD.

Some days, her thoughts raced faster than her feet. Other days, her motivation vanished mid-sentence. She made lists and forgot them. She showed up late but showed up big. She was loved, but rarely felt like enough.

During a month of burnout, Tasnim canceled everything. It was a personal retreat. A space to breathe and recalibrate. With God as her company, she whispered:

> Ya Hayyu Ya Qayyum, birahmatika astagheeth,
> aslih li sha'ni kullahu, wa la takilni ila nafsi
> wa la ila ahadin min khalqeka tarfata 'ayn.
>
> *Oh Lord, You are the Ever-Living, the One who*
> *sustains everything. I'm leaning on Your mercy.*
> *Please help me. Make things right in every part of*
> *my life, and don't leave me to myself or to anyone*
> *from Your creation, not even for a blink.*

She said it again. Then again. No deadlines. No speeches. Just a prayer to be sustained. Slowly, she began to breathe differently. She didn't fix everything overnight. In time, she began asking for help. She began forgiving her own pace.

For Tasnim, this dhikr was no longer an emergency exit. It became a daily doorway. A return to mercy, not perfection.

❀ The Habit-Breaker's Healing

Imran carried habits he couldn't quite shake. Small ones. Lingering ones. Some carved into routine, others born out of loneliness. Each time he promised change, a few weeks later he'd find himself circling back to old patterns. Then came the guilt, the shame, the self-doubt. Why am I like this? Why can't I stay consistent?

He didn't need lectures. He needed mercy.

One night, after another failed attempt at self-improvement, Imran sat on his prayer mat. Not to strategize, but to surrender. He whispered:

> Ya Hayyu Ya Qayyum, birahmatika astagheeth,
> aslih li sha'ni kullahu, wa la takilni ila nafsi
> wa la ila ahadin min khalqeka tarfata 'ayn.
>
> *Oh Lord, You are the Ever-Living, the One who
> sustains everything. I'm leaning on Your mercy.
> Please help me. Make things right in every part of
> my life, and don't leave me to myself or to anyone
> from Your creation, not even for a blink.*

He kept whispering it, slowly and often, like something his heart needed to hear.

Something changed. Not instantly, but quietly. He began repeating the dhikr each morning before temptation arrived, then again each night after the day's stumbles. It didn't erase the struggle. It gave the struggle a place to rest. A place to be seen. A place to heal.

For Imran, this dhikr became his private form of spiritual therapy. Not a perfect solution, but a persistent reminder that he was not alone. He was never too broken to be helped.

❀ When the Noise Faded

Aslam didn't grow up distant from faith. Her parents prayed. Her home was filled with reminders of God's mercy. Islam was practiced with subtle consistency. It was part of the backdrop of her childhood, familiar and comforting.

When she started university, everything shifted. She found herself drawn into new circles, new ways of being. At first, it felt exciting, to be seen, to be wanted, to be part of something new.

But slowly, the thrill turned into noise. The kind of noise that drowns out your own voice and leaves you wondering why you feel so far from yourself, from God.

One night, after another late night outing that left her feeling more drained than alive, Aslam sat alone in her room, crying. She sat still, lost in thought, wondering how she had come to feel so hollow. It hadn't happened all at once. It was a slow unraveling, an unspoken truth, a whisper in her chest that told her she wasn't made for this double identity. She didn't feel angry. Just tired. Tired of pretending. Tired of chasing a version of herself that never felt true.

And then she remembered a dhikr. She didn't understand every word, but she understood the feeling. The surrender. The softness. The plea.

Ya Hayyu Ya Qayyum, birahmatika astagheeth, aslih li sha'ni kullahu, wa la takilni ila nafsi wa la ila ahadin min khalqeka tarfata 'ayn.

Oh Lord, You are the Ever-Living, the One who sustains everything. I'm leaning on Your mercy. Please help me. Make things right in every part of my life, and don't leave me to myself or to anyone from Your creation, not even for a blink.

Aslam began to say it every morning, with intention, seeking understanding, protection, and return. Slowly, something began to shift. Not loudly. Not all at once. Just enough to feel like layers were falling away, leaving her closer to her essence. Her circles grew smaller, quieter, and in that narrowing, she found herself drawing closer to Allah.

❊ · ❊ · ❊

Dear Friend

This dhikr is not weakness. It's wisdom. It's the strength to say, "I cannot carry this alone," and the faith to believe in You, that I don't have to.

Say it when bad habits feel louder than your intentions. Say it when you feel targeted by others and the hurt finds no voice. Say it when you're too tired to be strong. Say it when your heart whispers, "Please take over."

Let yourself be present.
Take a deep breath.
And begin:

> Hi God, it's me again. I'm tired. I'm unsure. Please, don't leave me to myself, not even for a blink. I'm not asking for all the answers. Just presence. Just You. Sit with me in this fragile moment. Hold what I can't heal. Lift the burden I've held in silence. If I stumble again tomorrow, remind me that grace still covers me. That You're still here. Still listening.

I submit to You and I declare:

> Ya Hayyu Ya Qayyum, birahmatika astagheeth,
> aslih li sha'ni kullahu, wa la takilni ila nafsi
> wa la ila ahadin min khalqeka tarfata 'ayn.

> *Oh Lord, You are the Ever-Living, the One who sustains everything. I'm leaning on Your mercy. Please help me. Make things right in every part of my life, and don't leave me to myself or to anyone from Your creation ,not even for a blink.*

Chapter 15
Just You, God

Qul huwa Allahu aḥad.
Allahu aṣ-ṣamad.
Lam yalid wa lam yūlad.
Wa lam yakun lahu kufuwan aḥad.

You are One, God.
Steady and whole.
You were not born, and You do not
begin life as we do.
There is no one like You.
Not even close.

Dear Friend

There are days when your heart longs to reconnect. Not through answers. Not through complexity. Just through truth.

You might find yourself reaching for something simple. Something certain. Something that reminds you that God remains God, and you remain held.

Surat al-Ikhlāṣ is that reminder. It doesn't elaborate. It simply affirms. It whispers what your soul already knows: That Allah is One. Eternal. Beyond need. Beyond match.

> Qul huwa Allahu aḥad.
> Allahu aṣ-ṣamad.
> Lam yalid wa lam yūlad.
> Wa lam yakun lahu kufuwan aḥad.
>
> *You are One, God.*
> *Steady and whole.*
> *You were not born, and You do not begin life as we do.*
> *There is no one like You. Not even close.*

It's the heart of Oneness held within four verses. A declaration so powerful, the Prophet ﷺ described it as equal to one-third of the Quran.

Surat al-Ikhlāṣ is your spiritual exhale. It's the surah you say when the world feels complicated but you long for clarity. It's the one that returns you to the beginning. Not just of faith, but of trust.

Say it when you wake up feeling spiritually scattered or unfocused, or when doubts creep in and you need something simple to hold. Say it when you feel spiritually connected, when your heart is full of hope, or when confidence moves through you like light. Whatever space you're in, let it be something you can reach for.

❂ At Her Feet

Dawud is his mother Nafisah's caregiver and companion. Her body had slowed with time. Her memory dimmed in places. Her soul, though, glowed with a kind of light that even forgetfulness could not dim.

They live together in a beautiful, humble home. In every room, a prayer rug is placed with care. Each one offers an invitation to pause in thankfulness. Tasbih beads rest nearby, and a sense of shared devotion fills the air.

Each day, between pill schedules and slow breaths, they shared a sacred rhythm. Surat al-Ikhlāṣ, recited together thirty-three times. Sometimes in the car on the way to appointments. Sometimes in the kitchen while the tea steeped. Sometimes at night, right before sleep. Nafisah tucked into her favorite armchair, Dawud sitting at her feet:

> Qul huwa Allahu aḥad.
> Allahu aṣ-ṣamad.
> Lam yalid wa lam yūlad.
> Wa lam yakun lahu kufuwan aḥad.

> *You are One, God.*
> *Steady and whole.*
> *You were not born, and You do not begin life as we do.*
> *There is no one like You. Not even close.*

They didn't always finish in one sitting. Fatigue interrupted. Life distracted. That didn't matter. What mattered was the breath, the return, the shared remembrance.

Dawud once asked his mother where she learned to love this surah so deeply. She said, "Because it reminds me that I am not alone. Never alone. It reminds me of the One who never forgets me."

Over time, the recitation became less about habit and more about healing. For Nafisah, each repetition felt like placing a small pebble of devotion beneath the Throne. It marked her place in the Hereafter with whispered love. For Dawud, it balanced his soul. It was not just dhikr. It was shelter. It was home.

✦ Beyond Time, Beyond Grief

Hussein stood quietly at his brother's grave. The air was still. The sky pale. No words came easily.

They used to pray together. Laugh together. Recite Quran together, especially *Surat al-Ikhlāṣ* before sleep. "Three times," his brother would say. "Protection for the night."

Now, Hussein recited it alone. Not entirely. He believed it reached beyond time. Beyond the grave. Beyond grief.

> Qul huwa Allahu aḥad.
> Allahu aṣ-ṣamad.
> Lam yalid wa lam yūlad.
> Wa lam yakun lahu kufuwan aḥad.
>
> *You are One, God.*
> *Steady and whole.*
> *You were not born, and You do not begin life as we do.*
> *There is no one like You. Not even close.*

It didn't take away the ache. It did, however, remind him of eternal things. That God is still present. That God is still one. That God is still enough.

For Hussein, the surah became a companion. Not just protection from things unseen, but comfort for what had been lost. A small prayer. A big mercy.

❀ Good Night God

Omar was seven when he first learned Surat al-Ikhlāṣ. His grandfather didn't explain it. He simply recited it, slowly and gently, during each prayer. He never asked Omar to memorize it, but the way he repeated it felt like an invitation. As if he hoped the verses would settle somewhere deep, ready to rise when Omar needed them.

> Qul huwa Allahu aḥad.
> Allahu aṣ-ṣamad.
> Lam yalid wa lam yūlad.
> Wa lam yakun lahu kufuwan aḥad.

> *You are One, God.*
> *Steady and whole.*
> *You were not born, and You do not begin life as we do.*
> *There is no one like You. Not even close.*

He didn't realize it then, but those whispered prayers were shaping something tender inside him. A way of listening. A way of speaking. Over time, the flow of those verses began to echo in his own nightly voice.

Each evening, before Omar went to sleep, he escaped to a spiritual realm and found himself having one-to-one personal conversations with God. Although he did most of the talking, he knew deep down inside that God spoke back. He told Him everything. Who he sat beside. What made him smile. What made him small. His words came in run-on sentences and half-thoughts, the kind that tumbled out when his heart was full and his guard was down.

He always spoke in a whisper. Not to hide, but to keep the moment his. Sometimes he giggled, especially when he remembered something silly. Other times he cried, his voice trembling as he asked God why some moments felt so heavy.

Just as every chapter finds its closing lines, each time Omar parted from his conversation with God, he would end with Surat al-Ikhlāṣ. Then, in a whisper only God could hear, he would say, "Good night God. I love You."

❀ · ❀ · ❀

Dear Friend,

There is something timeless about returning to what is simple. A verse repeated in the kitchen. A prayer whispered at a graveside. A child's voice rising into sacred space.

Surat al-Ikhlāṣ is not long. It simply offers a stillness. A reminder. That God is One. Eternal. Steady. Whole.

Whether you are sitting beside someone you love, standing in grief, or lying in bed with your heart wide open, this surah remains. It meets you in silence. It meets you in longing. It meets you in love.

So if today feels heavy, or if today feels light, if you are reaching or resting, let it rise from within you. Let it be your rhythm. Let it be your return.

Let yourself be present.
Take a deep breath.
And begin:

> Hi God, it is me again.
> I don't always have the right words.
> Sometimes I come to You tired.
> Sometimes I come to You grieving.
> Sometimes I come to You full of wonder.
> But I come to You.
> And I will never stop.

I submit to You and I declare:

Qul huwa Allahu aḥad.
Allahu aṣ-ṣamad.
Lam yalid wa lam yūlad.
Wa lam yakun lahu kufuwan aḥad.

You are One, God.
Steady and whole.
You were not born, and You do not begin life as we do.
There is no one like You. Not even close.

Chapter 16
The Way Back

La ilaha illa anta
Subhanaka
inni kuntu mina al-dhalimin

There is no god but You. You are pure
and perfect. I have done wrong, hurting
myself in ways only You truly know. I
turn to You now, not with excuses, only
with hope. You are the One who
forgives, and I am the one in need.

Dear Friend,

There are moments in life when the weight of our own choices presses heavily on the heart. Regret can blur our vision. Shame can dim the voice that once reached out. We begin to wonder. Can I really turn back? Will I be accepted? Does mercy still reach me?

This dhikr is proof that it does.

> La ilaha illa anta
> Subhanaka
> inni kuntu mina al-dhalimin

> *There is no god but You. You are pure and perfect. I have done wrong, hurting myself in ways only You truly know. I turn to You now, not with excuses, only with hope. You are the One who forgives, and I am the one in need.*

It was spoken by Prophet Yunus ﷺ from the depths of a dark ocean, inside the belly of a whale. Utter isolation. Complete surrender. Yet it became his lifeline. It can be ours too.

Even the Prophet Muhammad ﷺ turned to God with humility, reminding us that seeking forgiveness is not a sign of weakness but of closeness.

This dhikr is an admission of humility, not hopelessness. It says, "God, I went off track. I lost my way. I still believe in You. I still trust in Your mercy." When you say it, you're not just confessing. You're returning.

Say it when guilt tries to consume you. Say it when you're overwhelmed by consequences. Say it when you're ready to stop running and begin healing.

⚙ Between Breaths, Between Tears

Tariq had been raised with the foundation of five daily prayers. It was woven into his childhood like breath. Natural. Unquestioned. In college, though, that tradition slipped into silence. Assignments blurred into late nights. Social circles expanded, and spaces for stillness became harder to find. He kept telling himself he'd start again. Tomorrow. Next week. Soon. The weeks turned into months, and the silence grew.

Then one morning, after a night that left him feeling hollow. Words spoken in anger. Choices he couldn't defend. He stepped outside. Not searching for clarity. Just air. He wandered into a small café near campus. At the counter, an elderly man fumbled with coins, apologizing softly for taking too long. The barista didn't snap. She just smiled and said, "Take your time. You're okay."

Tariq watched the exchange, something tightening in his chest. It was the way the man's apology was met with gentleness, not judgment. The way grace showed up in a moment that didn't demand it.

That evening, he whispered:

> La ilaha illa anta
> Subhanaka
> inni kuntu mina al-dhalimin

> *There is no god but You. You are pure and perfect. I have done wrong, hurting myself in ways only You truly know. I turn to You now, not with excuses, only with hope. You are the One who forgives, and I am the one in need.*

Not once, but again and again. Between breaths. Between tears. He began setting his alarm. One prayer a day. Then two. Then more. It wasn't perfect. It was honest.

Every sajdah felt like a return. Every whisper of the dhikr reminded him that mistakes don't disqualify us from mercy. They draw us toward it.

❋ The Broken Promise

Soraya had made a vow during Ramadan. No gossip. No backbiting. She had felt renewed, empowered. It only took one heated conversation. One moment of venting. The vow was broken. The words came out fast. Critical. Careless.

That night, Soraya couldn't sleep. Her conscience tugged at her. She remembered the verse about being held accountable for every word. She pulled out her prayer mat and whispered:

> La ilaha illa anta
> Subhanaka
> inni kuntu mina al-dhalimin

> *There is no god but You. You are pure and perfect. I have done wrong, hurting myself in ways only You truly know. I turn to You now, not with excuses, only with hope. You are the One who forgives, and I am the one in need.*

She didn't excuse herself. She didn't justify. She simply admitted and asked to be better.

From that day, Soraya started a private intention. One kind word a day to someone unexpected. A compliment. A note of thanks. A prayer for someone behind their back. Her words opened a path toward reconciliation. This dhikr became her compass.

❂ A Ribcage Prayer

Saleem hadn't spoken to his younger brother in three years. A bitter argument over inheritance had carved a canyon between them. Every Eid. Every family gathering. The silence throbbed.

Saleem told himself it was justified. That he was the wronged one. That silence was safer than reopening old wounds. Guilt, however, followed him like a shadow. It showed up in the silence between thoughts. In the pause before prayer. In the ache behind his chest when he heard his brother's name.

One day, in the middle of Friday Prayer, the Imam recited the dhikr of Yunus. Saleem felt like the verse was reaching directly into his ribcage. Not accusing. Just inviting.

> La ilaha illa anta
> Subhanaka
> inni kuntu mina al-dhalimin

> *There is no god but You. You are pure and perfect. I have done wrong, hurting myself in ways only You truly know. I turn to You now, not with excuses, only with hope. You are the One who forgives, and I am the one in need.*

He said it under his breath. Then again. Then louder. The words didn't fix everything. What they did was soften something deep within.

That night, he messaged his brother. No debate. No excuses. Just a simple note: If you're willing, I'd love to meet and talk. It was awkward. Painful. The first meeting unfolded gently, with long pauses and hesitant smiles. Just enough to let grace begin its work.

For Saleem, the dhikr didn't erase the past. It gave him courage to repair it. One conversation at a time. One prayer at a time.

❀ · ❀ · ❀

Dear Friend,

We all have moments we wish we could rewrite. Chapters marked by wrong turns, silence, or compromise.

This dhikr teaches us that the story isn't over. It's a lifeline whispered through tears. A rope thrown into the sea of guilt, pulling us toward the shore of mercy.

Say it when you feel unworthy. Say it when you don't know where to begin. Say it when you long for forgiveness but don't yet feel it.

Let yourself be present.
Take a deep breath.
And begin:

> Hi God, it's me again. I know I've made mistakes. I've drifted. I still believe in Your mercy. I still believe in Your perfection. I want to come back. Not perfectly. Just honestly. You know the depths of my darkness. You know my hidden secrets. You welcome me anyway. So I'm here, with all that I carry, asking to begin again.

I submit to You and I declare:

> La ilaha illa anta
> Subhanaka
> inni kuntu mina al-dhalimin

> *There is no god but You. You are pure and perfect. I have done wrong, hurting myself in ways only You truly know. I turn to You now, not with excuses, only with hope. You are the One who forgives, and I am the one in need.*

Chapter 17
Glory and Praise

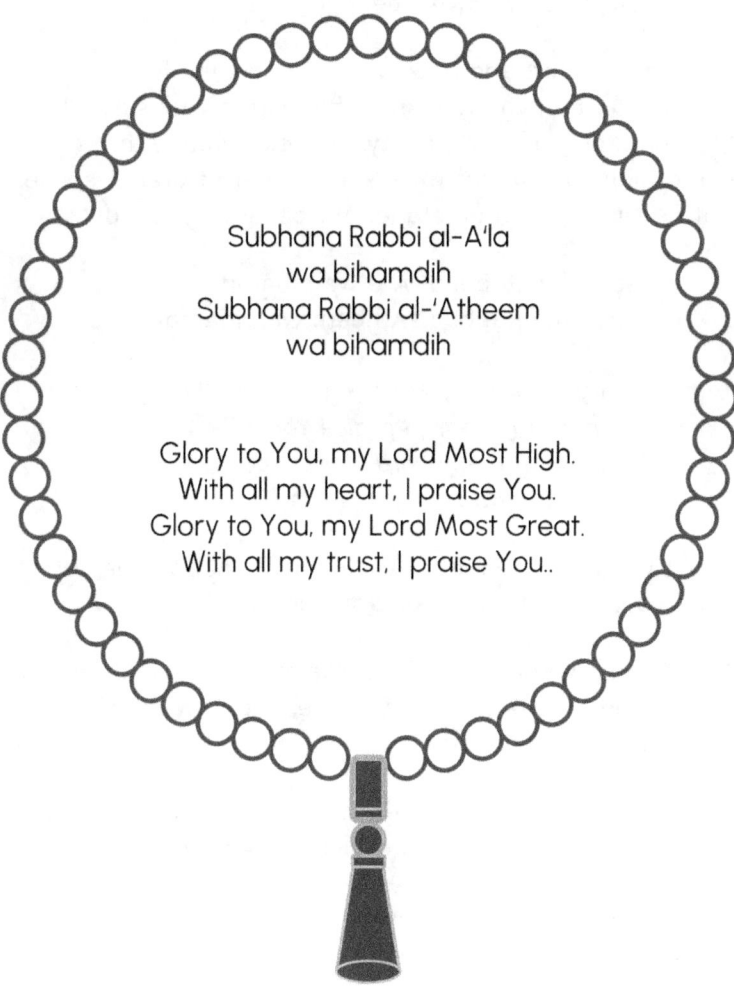

Subhana Rabbi al-A'la
wa bihamdih
Subhana Rabbi al-'Atheem
wa bihamdih

Glory to You, my Lord Most High.
With all my heart, I praise You.
Glory to You, my Lord Most Great.
With all my trust, I praise You..

Dear Friend,

Some prayers stand tall like minarets. Others bow low like the roots of an old olive tree.

This dhikr is soft and mighty all at once. It's for the moments when you feel small beneath a vast sky. When life humbles you with beauty, or breaks you with something you cannot fix. It's a whisper of praise, spoken not because you understand, but because you trust.

> Subhana Rabbi al-A'la wa bihamdih
> Subhana Rabbi al-'Atheem wa bihamdih
>
> *Glory to You, my Lord Most High.*
> *With all my heart, I praise You.*
> *Glory to You, my Lord Most Great.*
> *With all my trust, I praise You.*

Say it when you cannot change what is happening. When even your breath feels like a prayer.

Say it when you are staring at the stars, and something in you remembers how small you are, and how deeply held you still might be.

Say it when you are in awe of an ant's journey, carrying more than its weight, yet never turning away.

Say it when praise feels heavier than a plea, and your voice trembles, but your heart still believes.

And remember, these words were whispered by Prophet Muhammad ﷺ himself, in the grace of his bow and the stillness of his surrender.

❀ Cradle of Praise

Yaqub's workshop smelled of cedar, memory, and humility. He was building a cradle for his granddaughter. Not for sale. Just to cradle generations.

Each groove in the wood felt like prayer. He didn't use machines. Just his hands, a few old tools, and a dhikr that flowed from the soul.

> Subhana Rabbi al-A'la wa bihamdih
> Subhana Rabbi al-'Atheem wa bihamdih
>
> *Glory to You, my Lord Most High.*
> *With all my heart, I praise You.*
> *Glory to You, my Lord Most Great.*
> *With all my trust, I praise You.*

He wasn't trying to impress anyone. He was trying to honor the design, the grain, the timber, the moment, and the praise owed to the One who is only deserving of it.

His father had taught him to treat wood as sacred, because it, too, was from God. Now, Yaqub whispered praise with each stroke. Not to control the outcome. Just to surrender to something higher.

At one point, he paused mid-stroke. Not to correct a flaw, but to feel the stillness. The wood, the breath, the dhikr were all aligned in surrender, drawn toward presence. He closed his eyes for a moment, letting the silence shape him as much as he shaped the cradle.

By sunset, the cradle stood finished. Yaqub rested his hand on the wood and whispered the praise once more, letting the silence return it to God.

✹ The Sound of Healing

Khadija stood beside her mother's hospital bed. Monitors blinked softly. The air was sterile and slow. She didn't know what healing looked like anymore. Her prayers had turned from words to whispers.

She took her mother's hand and began to quietly repeat:

> Subhana Rabbi al-A'la wa bihamdih
> Subhana Rabbi al-'Atheem wa bihamdih
>
> *Glory to You, my Lord Most High.*
> *With all my heart, I praise You.*
> *Glory to You, my Lord Most Great.*
> *With all my trust, I praise You.*

Light as breath. Gentle as faith. It was praise. It was surrender.

She wasn't asking for anything. She was returning to the gentle trust that God is enough. To the surrender that remembers Allah is Great even when nothing makes sense.

In that moment of return, her heart softened. The fear didn't vanish. Something within her came to rest.

Because sometimes, healing begins with letting go.

✹ Glory in the Garden

Mama Rasmieh's garden was simple. It was sacred, too.

Roses bloomed in neat rows beside mint, basil, and a small patch of vegetables. The soil was dark and generous, as if it had been listening for years.

Each morning, she stepped into the garden with intention. She watered, she trimmed, she whispered:

> Subhana Rabbi al-A'la wa bihamdih
> Subhana Rabbi al-'Atheem wa bihamdih

> *Glory to You, my Lord Most High.*
> *With all my heart, I praise You.*
> *Glory to You, my Lord Most Great.*
> *With all my trust, I praise You.*

She didn't garden for routine. It was part of her daily conversation with the Most High. With every leaf she touched, she glorified the One who causes all things to grow.

Even the birds were drawn to her, as if the garden's praise had become a melody they recognized.

Her youngest son watched from the outdoor patio. He didn't speak. He simply observed. How she moved. How she whispered. How the garden seemed to respond. The echo of her praise lingered in the air, soft and steady, like something sacred being shared without words. It stayed with him.

The next morning, he stepped into the garden beside her. No phone. No rush. Just presence.

And the whisper became his too.

> Subhana Rabbi al-A'la wa bihamdih
> Subhana Rabbi al-'Atheem wa bihamdih

> *Glory to You, my Lord Most High.*
> *With all my heart, I praise You.*
> *Glory to You, my Lord Most Great.*
> *With all my trust, I praise You.*

❄ · ❄ · ❄

Dear Friend,

This dhikr is a soft return. Not rushed. Not forced. Just a leaning back with trust into the truth that God is still here. Still Great. Still worthy of every praise, even when the path feels uncertain.

It's the kind of trust that doesn't need to prove itself. The kind that shows up in gardens, in woodwork, in whispered breath. It's not loud, but it's steady. It reminds you that you don't have to understand everything to keep praising.

Say it when you feel unsure. Say it when you're tired of waiting. Say it when you're planting seeds you may never see bloom. Say it when you feel the warmth of something growing inside you. Something rooted in faith, not fear.

Let yourself be present.
Take a deep breath.
And begin:

> Hi God, it's me again. I don't have answers today. I have breath. I have praise. I carry this gentle trust that You are still growing something good. Even here. Even now. I may not see it clearly, but I believe it's unfolding. So, I'll stay close. I'll keep showing up with what I have.

I submit to You and I declare:

> Subhana Rabbi al-A'la wa bihamdih
> Subhana Rabbi al-'Atheem wa bihamdih
>
> *Glory to You, my Lord Most High.*
> *With all my heart, I praise You.*
> *Glory to You, my Lord Most Great.*
> *With all my trust, I praise You.*

Letter to the Reader

Dear Friend,

Thank you for allowing this book to walk beside you on your sacred journey. It was written with care. Not to instruct, but to accompany. To offer present companionship in moments of reflection, longing, growth, and healing. Whether you arrived with questions, hopes, or came seeking a moment to breathe, I hope these pages met you with gentleness and grace.

If these pages have offered you something practical to carry into your daily life, I'm grateful. The practices shared here are simple invitations. They are meant to be adapted, embraced, or returned to whenever your heart feels ready. There is no right pace. No need for perfection. Only the gentle unfolding of your own path.

If you found your story reflected in these pages, or even a single moment that felt familiar, I hope you'll consider sharing this book with someone you love. A friend. A sibling. A parent. A child. Sometimes, the gentlest words are the ones we pass along. Often, we're more connected than we realize. A single sentence can soften a heart. A shared prayer can remind someone they're not alone. What speaks to you might be exactly what someone else has been waiting to hear.

My hope is that this book becomes a companion to your heart. May it offer comfort when you need it. Clarity when you seek it. A sense of belonging that reaches beyond the page. If it has spoken to you, even in a small way, then it has fulfilled its purpose.

More than anything, I hope this book encourages you to build, rebuild, or gently strengthen your relationship with God. Your eternal Friend. Always near. Always listening. Whether through prayer, remembrance, or quiet moments of honesty, may you feel held in that closeness. And may you never forget. God loves you, and has always loved you. That love is constant. Gentle. Vast. It waits not for perfection, but for presence.

With gratitude and peace,
Brother Reza

Let yourself be present.
Take a deep breath.
And begin:

Hi God, it is me again...

www.ingramcontent.com/pod-product-compliance
Lightning Source LLC
Chambersburg PA
CBHW070342130626
46556CB00007B/2992